# The Crooked Path to Victory

WHAT PROFITETH IT?

# The
# Crooked Path
# to Victory

## Drugs and Cheating in
## Professional Bicycle Racing

# Les Woodland

Cycle Publishing / Van der Plas Publications, San Francisco

Copyright Les Woodland, 2003

Printed in U.S.A.

## Published by:

Cycle Publishing (formerly Van der Plas Publications)
1282 7th Avenue
San Francisco, CA 94122, U.S.A.
Tel:         (415) 665-8214
Fax:         (415) 753-8572
E-mail:    pubrel@cyclepublishing.com
Web site:  http://www.cyclepublishing.com

## Distributed or represented to the book trade by:

| | |
|---|---|
| USA: | Midpoint Trade Books, Kansas City, KS |
| Canada: | New Society Publishers, Gabriola Island, BC |
| Great Britain: | Orca Book Services / Chris Lloyd Sales and Marketing Services, Poole |
| Australia: | Tower Books, Frenchs Forest, NSW |

| | |
|---|---|
| Cover design: | Kent Lytle, Alameda, CA |
| Frontispiece: | Cartoon illustration about early six-day racing that appeared in the *New York Herald*, 1897 |

Cataloging in Publication Data
Woodland, Les, 1947—
The Crooked Path to Victory: Drugs and Cheating in Professional Bicycle Racing.
p. 22.6 cm. Includes bibliographic information and index.
1. Bicycle Racing; I. Authorship; II. Title.
ISBN 1-892495-40-6 (paperback original); 1-892495-90-2 (digital edition)
Library of Congress Control Number 2003105927

# Table of Contents

# About the Author

Les Woodland has spent over thirty years writing about cycling, something his mother insisted was no job for a grown man.

These days, he writes mainly for English publications, but his work also appears in the US. In the early days of the US cycle racing bi-weekly *Velo-News*, he was a regular contributor to that publication.

His earlier books include *The Unknown Tour de France*, which was also published by Cycle Publishing / Van der Plas Publications and is still available both in the US and in Britain, as well as in a German edition.

He now lives permanently near Toulouse in France, where Englishmen who know about bicycle racing are as rare as Frenchmen who understand cricket. The thinning hair is due to worry about meeting his publisher's oppressive deadlines.

# 1. Choppy Waters

It would be convenient if more people would look like their stereotypes. Burglars should wear masks and striped jerseys and carry bags marked "swag"; all foreigners should be shifty and offer you postcards of their sister; boxers should never speak in long sentences or write books. Then we'd all know where we stand.

Luckily it was just that way with Choppy Warburton. He looked the part of the dubious guru, the svengali of the track center, with all-knowing smiles and a taste for long overcoats and curly-brimmed hats. His mouth was broad and topped by a curving mustache. His legs "never end," as *Paris Vélo* put it. To this day, nobody seems to know just what his methods were — whether he used drugs, magic, or smoke-and-mirrors. Fact is, his riders went extraordinarily well but often died young and usually miserably.

Warburton's record includes the death of a classics winner, the wreck of a world sprint champion… and being banned for life. He was either cycling's first great dope king or a magnificent confidence trickster. Either way, there is blood on his hands.

Choppy, of course, wasn't his real name. His family called him James and he came from Haslingden in Lancashire, in northern England. Its faded celebrity now is that it's home to one of Britain's most prominent meat-pie makers, but in earlier days its quarries provided the stone to build Trafalgar Square in London.

"Choppy" had been the nickname of a seagoing uncle whose contempt for the wildest seas let him admit only that it was "a little choppy out there."

James liked the name and the daredevil image, and he borrowed both for himself when he set about making a reputation as a runner. He was good at running, too, and he became a professional in the roughhouse of the "pedestrian" world of northern England, where runners competed for cash at miners' galas and not infrequently rigged the results between them.

We're talking now about the late 19th century, a time when "amateur" in English-speaking countries meant what it said, a competitor who competed just for *amour*, the love of competition, and certainly not for money. Most amateur sports excluded each other's professionals, so Warburton never became a rider when he interested himself in cycling. If he had, it would have been in the equally wild style of unregistered professionalism, where riders competed on unbanked grass tracks in the north of England for cash prizes. Moving from running to cycling was easy, because the same body, the Amateur Athletic Association, governed both sports in Britain until cycling found the confidence to go alone with the foundation of the Bicycle Union in 1878.

The agreement to keep out every other sport's professionals may have stopped Warburton racing on the track itself, but it couldn't keep him out of the track center. And there he entranced riders like a snake. His fame spread

Choppy Warburton with some of his best-known charges, from left to right: Arthur Linton, Choppy, in hat and overcoat, Jimmy Michael, and Tom Linton.

so well that the *Cycling Gazette* of Chicago described him as "undoubtedly the most widely-advertised figure in European cycle-racing circles; his every movement created talk."

The track director Tristan Bernard pointed him out to Toulouse-Lautrec, the post-impressionist painter. The ugly old alcoholic was equally fascinated, and painted him at work. Bernard, incidentally, is said to have been the man who hit on the idea of ringing a bell to indicate the last lap. It had never happened before, in any sport, until he started it at the Buffalo and Vélodrome de la Seine tracks in Paris, which he directed.

*Paris-Vélo* was equally impressed by Warburton and said approvingly, "He is everywhere at the same time, never in the same place. In the track center he is the only one you see, his great overcoat and his derby hat pushed down to his ears with a bang of his fist. He gives out an air of mystery that intrigues rivals and thrills the public."

He would, the French reporters said, race from one side of the track to the other to urge on his riders.

"From his pocket he suddenly takes a small glass container, shows it to his rider, uncorks it with dramatic care, pours the unknown mixture that it contains into a milk bottle and, still running, knocking over anyone who gets in the way, gets himself to the other side of the track to pass it to Linton." That would have been Arthur Linton, who will shortly make a further appearance in this story. He too died in misery, like so many of Warburton's other protégés.

"It's a drug, say some, just bluff say others," *Paris-Vélo* continued, "but drug or bluff, it's all the same. Choppy will always be able to say that he managed four riders and made champions of three of them: Arthur and Tom Linton, James Michael, and Albert Champion."

Arthur Linton was born in 1872 in Wales, where he and his brothers Samuel and Thomas joined the Aberdare cycling club, founded in 1884. The club also produced Jimmy Michael, a tiny sprinter who also died in miserable circumstances as we will see as the story progresses.

Samuel was originally the best of the three, especially over short distances, but by 1892 Arthur and Thomas had eclipsed him, beating record after record in Britain and on the Continent.

Arthur liked to emphasize his Welsh origins, often riding in a pale blue jersey embroidered with the crest of the Prince of Wales. He was a long-distance rider, which meant he raced on the road. The sport was divided between track competitors — of whom the most glamorous were the sprinters and the most daredevil the pace-followers behind their teams of tandems or even motorbikes — and road racers. There were some fearsome endurance races on the track, but they were just part of a wider program. By contrast, road races were always trials of endurance. The further the race, the greater the superhuman ability the riders needed, and the more the newspaper promoting the race could boast of the giants it had engaged. It was an era, after all, when most people did not travel much beyond their village.

To run a race between two cities with a long distance between them had two benefits: It brought home the sheer excess of the task the riders faced, and it sold more papers. There was no radio or television. News spread only through gossip or by newspapers, which were free to boast their claims as they wished. So, having created an appetite and excitement for their races, they could then look forward to increased sales in every village the race passed, as people tried to work out what had happened.

The start of the first Bordeaux–Paris race in 1891.

The race that appealed to Arthur Linton was Bordeaux–Paris, from the port city on the southwest coast to the capital — almost 600 km away. It was started in 1891 by *Véloce-Sport*, one of many papers of the era that mixed sports reporting with politics and passionate views. The race was so popular that it inspired the rival paper *Le Petit Journal* to organize a similarly brutal marathon race, Paris–Brest–Paris, that same year.

Bordeaux–Paris was popular because it was such an extraordinarily long way. It was so far that the organizers of the Vélo Club Bordeaux thought it would take two or three days, and laid on beds and meals along the course. To their surprise, visiting British amateurs took the first four places without sleeping, the bike factory manager George Mills winning in 26 hours. To put that in perspective, he had gone half the speed of the express train between the two cities. And when Louis Mottiat won the startling Bordeaux–Paris–*and back* in 1920, he did it in 56 hours — an average less than Mills had managed on his primitive bike almost three decades before.

Mills' success encouraged other British riders, not least Linton. He reported to the start on the evening of Saturday 23 May 1896, and set off in bat-

Gaston Rivierre, winner of the 1891 Bordeaux–Paris race.

tle with the nattily-bearded Frenchman Gaston Rivierre. Their battle, paced by tandems manned by three and sometimes four men, produced a record speed. They averaged 27.7 km/h, which may be slow for a modern race, but still pretty fast for 591 km on roads of compacted and rutted mud. At the time, cobbles weren't an inconvenience: they were the state of the art.

Although perhaps with some illicit help… A report in *Cyclers' News* "by one who knows" says:

> I saw him at Tours, half-way through the race, at midnight, where he came in with glassy eyes and tottering limbs, and in a high state of nervous excitement. I then heard him swear — a very rare occurrence with him — but after a rest he was off again, though none of us expected he would go very far. At Orléans at five o'clock in the morning, Choppy and I looked after a wreck — a corpse, as Choppy called him — yet he had sufficient energy, heart, pluck, call it what you will, to enable him to gain 18 minutes on the last 45 miles of hilly road.

"Gain 18 minutes" because Linton had been passed along the way by Rivierre, a man who rode scrupulously to a schedule rather than engage in elbow-to-elbow battles with his opponents. In his glassy-eyed state, Linton may not even have registered that he was second rather than win the lead. If there was one volt left in his befuddled brain, he must have realized he had never caught Rivierre. And that therefore there was something odd about the appreciation and puzzled disappointment that the French crowd showed him when he got to Tristan Bernard's Vélodrome de la Seine. He seemed to have won. He had done two laps of the track by the time Rivierre arrived. Imagine the effort it must have taken to work that out after so many corpse-like hours.

The truth was that Rivierre — who went on to win Bordeaux-Paris again in 1897 and 1898 and died in 1942 — had been first to reach the Suresne valley on the approach to Paris. The course then made a loop through Courbevoie. Rivierre went the right way. Linton's pacers, though, took him along the Quai de Puteaux and across the Seine by the wrong bridge, which cut off some distance. The shortcut was minor compared to the total distance, so after a protest, the judges gave victory to both men and they shared first and second prizes. The officials were impressed at Linton's courage and, it was said, also feared the trouble they would get from the British if they demoted him. The third man, Marius Thé of France, arrived 55 minutes later. The last one didn't turn up for another day.

Linton was a hero in France and at home, but how had he done it? According to the writer Louis Minart, he had been in such an appallingly state that Warburton had abandoned him after Orléans and caught the first train to Paris. Even his sponsor, the chain maker Simpson who had provided his bike, wanted him to climb off. Rumors started to spread. *Sporting Life* reported: "I hear by a side wind that one eminent promoter of professionalism could a tale unfold which would cause each individual hair upon the Licensing Committee of the NCU to stand on end."

The National Cyclists' Union was the body that ran the sport in Britain, licensed riders and trainers, and drew up the rules. It had never been happy about Warburton, the runner turned svengali, and almost certainly the "promoter of professionalism" that *Sporting Life* was talking about.

*Sporting Life* had heard that Linton had been repeatedly dosed with strychnine, trimethyl, or heroin — possibly in combinations of two or more. It had no proof, and there were certainly no tests. But all three drugs were common at Six Day races, where some riders were drugged so heavily that they thought they were nailed to the track or chased by knifemen.

That was May. In June, Linton returned to Britain to ride the Great Chain Match at Catford. Today, Catford is a rather ordinary suburb of southeast London, but in 1896 it was a leafy place where the comfortable middle-class lived — rather different from today. A bunch of teenagers, led by a C. P. Sisley, started a club there in April 1886, and it prospered and soon had branches in Bristol, Cardiff, Nottingham, and even Paris. Its membership brought in considerable sums in annual fees. The financial acumen that made that possible encouraged the club to build a track after it realized how much profit could be made if they could charge the people who had been turning out to watch their races on the road.

Catford track was considered the fastest in Europe, with seats for 1,000. The surface was topped with concrete to give a better grip to the pneumatic tires that the riders were just starting to use. There was an exciting innovation, a banking in the turns that increased the speed. The view, until entrepreneurs spoiled it by building houses, was of rolling green hills in one direction and the edges of London in the other.

You can still make out where it was from the street names; find the South Circular Road as it winds through the southern suburbs just east of Catford and Catford Bridge railroad stations, turn off into Laleham Road and then take the second left and you'll be in Sportsbank Road. That's where spectators stood when they couldn't get a seat.

The Great Chain Match was a commercial challenge between the company that made the "Simpson Lever Chain," and sponsored Linton in Bordeaux–Paris, and those that made conventional chains — the sort still used today. Simpson's chains came up with a chain that was described as having leverage in the links and the manufacturer was prepared to spend a fortune proving its superiority. This was an era characterized by rapid innovation (and more than a few hoaxes and fallacies — which applied in the case of the Simpson Lever Chain) in the bicycle industry.

I interviewed a man called Harry Carrington. He was born in 1910, ten years after the track was torn down, a victim of bungled finances. He was 92, although he sounded 20 years younger, and apologized dryly for "not getting out cycling much these days." He had been a member of the Catford for 57 years.

"The chain companies paid untold sums to prove their point," he said. "It defeated the whole purpose because money bought you pacing teams, and those who bought the best pacer won the race. The Simpson people brought over the Gladiator pacers from Paris, and they were just that much better than

Advertising poster for the Simpson Chain company, which sponsored the Catford Chain Match.

the Dunlop team, and so Simpson won the match. But who's heard of Simpson and his invention now?

In fact, two of the three Simpson riders won their race but, as Harry said, what good dit it do? Did it really prove that Simpson's chains were superior or rather that the riders were superior?

The Catford Chain Race attracted thousands of spectators. "Pacers were strong, experienced racing cyclists, most of whom were ambitious to become stars themselves. (…) Four or five strong riders working together on one of these large cumbersome machines were extremely fast and powerful," says the historian Andrew Ritchie. They were there along with at least two World Champions, a team of Americans to ride the supporting events, a dubious American agent, and Warburton, the equally doubtful British one. Plus those "untold sums."

The top draw was a tiny Welshman called Jimmy Michael, just five feet tall and weighing 100 lb. He looked like a 15-year-old. Michael was one of Britain's first World Champions, having won the 1895 100-km motor-paced title by leaving the silver-medallist, Luyten of Belgium, at four kilometers.

Michael's "childlike face topped a body lightly sloped forwards and always motionless; only his legs moved and turned madly at the greatest speeds," said one report. Paced racing was a huge attraction, and Michael was one of its brightest stars from 1895 to 1899 who made a fortune — certainly more than a boy from a poor Welsh coal-mining village would ever have thought possible. And enough to attract the attention of Choppy Warburton.

The Catford promoters pitched Michael in a series of races against Charley Barden, silver medallist in the professional sprint the following year in Copenhagen. A pace-follower against a sprinter: an edgy match over different distances, or one that could be billed that way anyway.

The climax came in the five-miler. The two men took off their warm-up clothing and began toying with their bikes. The excitement in the stand was enormous. The outcome depended as much on mental as physical strength, and at one time Michael, who had just been offered a series of races in America and wanted to impress, was seen to walk over to Warburton. It could have been to bluff, to prepare, or to cheat — nobody knows.

The two talked briefly and Warburton nodded, smiled, and reached into his overcoat for a small bottle. Michael reached for it and took a drink.

Exactly what happened next has been lost. It's not even entirely certain whether it happened at Catford or at another Chain Race, in Germany. All we know is that it happened, that Warburton and Michael were at the center of it all. Stories range from Michael being simply but surprisingly beaten to his spinning off his bike and then, dizzy and uncomprehending, getting back on and riding off in the wrong direction. What the reports agree on is that the crowd yelled "Dope!"

Now, dope these days means a stimulant, something to make you go faster. At the time, though, it was more commonly meant as something intended to make a human, or more usually a horse, go slower. The mixed reports of Michael's behavior could mean either. But, as the Six Day races showed, spectators weren't averse to seeing competitors make fools of themselves. If Michael went berserk and rode off the wrong way, it would disappoint purists

## Whatever Happened to... Albert Champion?

Champion, who was another of Choppy War burton's stable, was born in Paris on 5 April 1878. He won Paris–Roubaix in 1899 and moved to the USA in 1900, having already ridden races there. He was 21 and married, but the marriage failed and he married a show-business girl in 1922. He started his spark-plug company on capital of $5,000 with a pair of brothers in 1905 — motorcycles were his other passion — and by the time the great-grandchildren sold the company in 1989, it was worth $750 million.

Champion died in Paris on 26 October 1927, leaving his wife the then startling sum of $15 million.

The American historian Peter Nye, who is writing Champion's biography, says: "It was a classy final scene. He was being honored by automobile industry major domos from both sides of the Atlantic. They feted him for making the spark plugs that had kept Lindbergh's plane running on the aviator's solo flight across the Atlantic earlier that year. Albert collapsed at their feet.

"Published accounts said a heart attack killed him, age 49. My investigation indicates he was beaten up by his second wife's *amour*, who did the same to her."

who had hoped to see an exciting race, but it would have delighted the end of the market that liked a little sensation.

It's easy to see why Warburton would dope his man to go faster. He had a reputation for that, using the drugs of the time to increase the tension of tired muscles (strychnine) and to deaden the nerves (heroin). If Michael rode like a dying chicken, it was because he had been given too much of one or both.

But why would Warburton want him to lose? The answer here lies in the shady American agent who'd accompanied the Americans riding the support races. His name was Bliss, and it was he who had offered Michael the exhibition races across the Atlantic. Warburton wouldn't have wanted him to go. He'd not only lose a client but the prestige of looking after a champion. How convenient, then, to nobble Michael at one of the biggest meetings of the year, make a fool of him and kill his value to America.

Certainly Bliss consoled Michael on what had happened. One version of the story says he persuaded Michael to "admit" he had taken a drug, thereby explaining the mishap and maintaining his box-office appeal in America and also indicting Warburton. Michael said he'd agree if the contracts in America were honored, and indeed they were.

We shall probably never know the truth. All we know is that Linton was glassy-eyed and trembling, and that Michael was ill or crazy, and flopped out of a race which should have been the tightest of matches. The National Cyclists' Union needed no more. It banned Warburton from every track in Britain, a procedure known as warning-off. He left for Germany in 1897 and managed the Frenchman Albert Champion, an early classics winner and founder of the Champion spark plug company. He died in north London that same year, just before Christmas, aged 54.

And Michael? Well, he too died young. He was on his way to America on the liner *Savoie* in November 1904 for a last round of exhibition races in the hope of bringing order to the shipwreck of his life. The man who was once one of the richest athletes in the world was spiritually and financially broken, his money gone on horses and horse-racing. The trip to the U.S. was a last effort to square the books, to win self-respect and regain the admiration of others. It never happened. He died on board, just 28.

The cause of death was put at "fatigue fever." It certainly wasn't genetic: his brother Billy, who also toured the US and was never beaten in eight major matches and four exhibition meetings, was still giving interviews when he was 84.

Which leaves Linton. He died just nine weeks after Bordeaux-Paris of an affliction described as typhoid fever. It was 23 July 1896, and he was at home in Aberdare, Wales. His brothers, too, died of the same fever, and *Cyclers' News* on 28 July 1896 decided that "the gigantic effort Linton made in the Bordeaux to Paris race undermined his constitution, and gave him little strength to battle against the fever." Dr. E. B. Turner, "the Cycling Doctor," wrote:

> It seems that he rode in the Six Days' race at the Agricultural Hall [London] last March and he had not had a week's rest from long-distance competition. He took part in two all-day races on the road in France, in one of which, Paris–Bordeaux (*sic*) he was completely exhausted and beat the record by three hours.

Bryan Wotton, the former racing secretary of the British Cycling Federation (which replaced the NCU) and later doping adviser to the International Amateur Athletics Federation, says a man should be judged by his friends. "The chapter of incidents leading up to Linton's death and his close association with Warburton would seem to indicate that it probably partially resulted from the use of dope," he says.

Even the track didn't escape the wreckage. It lasted just five years and the money it lost all but crippled the club. Harry Carrington says:

> A syndicate opened the Herne Hill track about the same time and then the Crystal Palace track was rebuilt. The Boer War was on, there was general poverty, men were away in the army. There was too much competition for three tracks within a few miles of each other. And they leased the land with the condition, I suppose, that they returned it in the condition they got it in. So not only did building the track cost a fortune but running it lost another one and then demolishing it afterwards brought the club to its knees. It was generally a disaster.

We haven't reached the 20th Century yet, and already we have riders winning unbelievable sums, riders cheating, riders dying, riders disputing results, and riders falling prey to unqualified medical men. We haven't yet had riders openly cheating, selling each other victories, going to jail. But we will. Very soon.

# 2. Six-Day Wonders

Remember what "the Cycling Doctor" said about Linton riding the Six Day race at the Agricultural Hall in London? If ever there was an epicenter for shady men and dubious practices, it was the Six Day races of first London, then the United States, and after them the rest of the cycling world.

The idea of a six-day race was, and remains, very simple. Someone drops a flag at the start of six days and whoever rides furthest by the end of the week is the winner. It's got a bit more complicated and more humane since then, but that's the principle.

The races came out of a craze for marathon walks. I don't know if it was the first in the world, but the first one held at the Agricultural Hall in Islington, north London — where the world's first Six Day bike race was also held — was in April 1877. Edward Payson-Weston of the USA and Daniel O'Leary of Cork in Ireland bet each other £500 and set off to win the wager. The idea was to be the first to cover 500 miles, which O'Leary managed in 135 hours. Weston had walked "only" 478 miles. You'd think the two would have settled matters there and paid up. Instead, they started off again. The idea now was to see who would be the first to drop. It was Weston, after 510 miles. His Irish rival pocketed the money with 520 miles in his legs.

There was another race the following year, this time with 23 starters. Eighteen of them finished, a man called Conky winning with such a lead that before walking the last lap, he rested for an hour and changed his clothes. The crowd was impressed. The *Illustrated London News*, though, wrote: "It may be an advantage to know that a man can travel 520 miles in 138 hours, and manage to live through a week with an infinitesimal amount of rest, though we fail to perceive that anyone could possibly be placed in a position where his ability in this respect would be of any use to him [and] what is to be gained by a constant repetition of the fact."

Atrociously bad taste, then? You bet. And just right for cycling. If 20,000 people a day would pay to watch mere walkers, imagine how they would go wild at the speed of men on bicycles. That's what the promoters thought.

The Agricultural Hall is still there, although it's not called that these days. It's now the Business Design Centre, although from the facade you can still see the grand scale on which it was built. The front looks like a castle, with a huge arched brick doorway big enough to take the largest horses and carts or even royal carriages. Two high stories stretch to each side, both completed by a tower at least twice as high. Behind it rises an arch of iron and steel, like a great Victorian railroad station.

Islington has changed, too. It was on the very edge of London when the Duke of Bedford, Lords Somerville and Winchelsea, and Sir Joseph Banks dreamed of a huge agricultural show in 1778 and formed their Smithfield Club. Their farming bonanza has moved on since then, but it's still the largest in Britain. In 1862 it moved to the newly completed Agricultural Hall, of which one newspaper wrote that it "is well entitled to a place among the prominent features of institutions of the Metropolis." It was 312 feet long, 123 feet across and 72 feet at its highest.

The hall was so enormous that it had its own micro-climate. London was a stinking dirty city at the end of the 19th century with its many factories and workshops pouring smoke unrestricted into the area. Thick yellow fogs, a mixture of water vapor and pollution known as smog, weren't uncommon. They may look romantic in Jack-the-Ripper and Dickens films but they were lethal. Thousands died.

One of the killer fogs in 1874 collected under the curved roof of the Agricultural Hall and couldn't escape. There was a farming show at the time and the animals were reported to have died one by one as the mix of moisture and smoke crept down inch by inch from the ceiling. The people got out, but the cows suffocated. Only the pigs and sheep, which weren't as tall, escaped the cloudy death that descended towards them.

To be honest, I hadn't expected the hall still to be there. I thought it must long since have been pulled down, especially since Islington has moved from a village on the edge of London to an industrial inner-city suburb and then — in parts anyway — to a much-gentrified and prized and expensive place to live. On the British Monopoly board it's one of the cheapest sites to buy; in the real world, it certainly is not these days.

I started going through files to see what had become of the place, what they had to say about it, and there to my surprise I was staring at a modern photograph of the modern facade, smarter now than in Victorian times, but still obviously the home of Six Day bike racing. Far from dying and being pulled down — which it nearly was until the poet John Betjeman started a campaign in 1974 to save it — it stands in its own piazza with a Hilton hotel to one side.

The second surprise was to find that the man in charge of exhibitions there was a former professional cyclist. Mick Bennett, known as "Pretty Boy" in the bunch in those days for his youthful looks, was one of those talented all-rounders who could ride Six Days, win medals as an international team-pursuiter, ride classic road races on the Continent, and then manage teams.

He's silver-haired and thicker set than in those days, of course — a man-in-a-suit in his 50s — but still with enough a bike-rider's mischief to re-call with bitterness and pride that, alone among the team that won medals for Britain in the team pursuit at the Montreal Olympics, he had been the one to whom the Queen declined to give a medal.

To be honest, neither he nor I thought the Queen had any idea who Mick Bennett was. We doubted she realized there weren't three but four in a pursuit team. We laugh at the idea of her Little Girl voice protesting "But one hasn't seen the naughty one, has one?"

"Is that why you didn't get the letters after your name then?" I ask, "for being naughty?"

"For speaking my mind, really. It's a long time ago now [the 1970s], and in those days those in charge of the sport didn't approve of people who had the nerve to say what was wrong and to make suggestions, and I think that's why I got left out. I felt bitter at the time — I still do a bit, I suppose — but these days it just makes me smile."

We have lunch together in the canteen overlooking the arena where the first races happened and then go down to his office behind a smoked glass wall that reaches from floor to ceiling.

"Look at this," he says, pulling old black-and-white prints from a file. "Great, isn't it?"

The *Penny Illustrated Paper*, had produced a line engraving of a cyclist on a high-wheeled bicycle — a penny-farthing as they would have called them in Britain, from the smallest and largest coins of the era — with a small trailing wheel. He is wearing a long-sleeved buttoned vest, a peaked cap, surprisingly modern black shorts to mid-thigh, and shoes like casual slip-ons. His handlebars are curved like a World War One mustache and he's riding a shallow banked track edged by a low wall of upright posts and some sort of material, probably canvas. Above him hangs a horizontal wheel, the size of a cart wheel, topped by several dozen candles.

That much is interesting enough but alongside the man, on an earth trail circuiting the banking, is a man on a galloping horse. "Cowboy v. Cyclist at the Agricultural Hall," says the caption with the advice to "see 'Sport.'" The date: 19 November 1887. The era: clearly one of sensation above athleticism.

AGRICULTURAL HALL.
Monday, November 18th,
AND FIVE FOLLOWING DAYS.
MONSTER EXHIBITION
of
BICYCLES, TRICYCLES, & BICYCLING
APPLIANCES.
Gold, Silver, and Bronze Medals for best Roadster and Racing Bicycle- and Tricycle ; also Three Medals for Bicycling appliances.
For further particulars, plans of the hall, and terms for space, &c., for exhibiting, apply to ETHERINGTON & CO., Advertising Agents, East Temple Chambers, Whitefriars-street, E.C., or to Mr. Date, the Secretary of the Agricultural Hall Company, Islington, N.

GREAT SIX DAYS' BICYCLE RACE
FOR THE
CHAMPIONSHIP OF THE WORLD.
£150 in Prizes (First Prize, £100),
Which will be deposited in the hands of the *Sporting Life* to be given up to the winners.
Entries to be made to the *Sporting Life*, 148, Fleet-street, E.C., on or before November 12 together with an entrance fee of £1 1s., where all particulars respecting the race can be obtained.

Above: Advertisement for the first Six Day race in the Agricultural Hall, Islington.

Left: Cyclist versus horse race at Agricultural Hall. (Source: *Penny Illustrated Paper*)

We have a good laugh and carry on through a file of posters of bike shows and other races before arriving at the very thing I had been looking for: a picture of the world's first Six Day race. The banked track seems to have disappeared and so has the fencing, since the high-wheeled racers are now just riding between rows of well-dressed men in overcoats, only some of whom are actually watching the racing.

The riders have changed, too, because now they have tight pants with stockings pulled to their knees, and their handlebars are straight and narrow. The ornate and iron-fronted balconies sketched into the background are still there and I stood and gazed down at the arena as thousands must have done that week in November 1878.

The track was wooden and seven and a half laps to the mile. The original iron columns and ornate balustrades are still there. Pace them out and you can see the available area is about 45 by 130 meters. That's a pretty tiny area for a bike track you would circle for nearly a week.

But what had happened? How had the racing gone? Was there scandal and sensation or polite interest and a chilly walk home? There was nothing in the hall's files, so I walked through the streets for two or three miles until I found the right library for the suburb's old newspaper collection. And then, turning the primitive metal spool on the microfiche displays of the *Islington Gazette*, I found the report I wanted. The paper had given a lot less than it had to the pedestrian event, but it was an account, nevertheless, of the first Six Day bike race in the world.

"A bicycle contest was commenced at the Agricultural-hall, on Monday last," it started, "for which £150 is offered in prizes for a six days' competition, the money to be allotted thus: £100 for the first man, £25 for the second, £15 for the third, and £10 for the fourth." That was a good deal less than for the International Pedestrian Match Championship of the World ("a fair field and no favour, the best man to win; full military band") in which the winner got not only £500 but half the gate money as well.

£500 is about $800 these days, but comparisons are impossible over the years, not just because of inflation, but because expectations of how well people would live and the money they needed are so different. And anyway, how much would you want just to take part, which was far more than you could be making at a factory bench or a clerk's desk?

25

The race started at 6 AM on Monday, but only four of the field of 12 were on the line. The others joined in when they felt ready, the view being that this was a challenge of endurance rather than a man-to-man dash. The track was small and difficult and built by someone restricted not only by the narrow confines but a lack of any experience of track design. Spectators who climbed to the balconies therefore had a perfect view of the frequent crashes.

The *Islington Gazette* reported: "At seven o'clock Markham fell heavily, and ten minutes later the Frenchman [Terront] came on the track and rattled away in fine style, he at that time being 17 miles and a half behind the leader, Phillips. The men kept well together for some time after this, but at twenty minutes past nine Markham again came to grief, Andrews falling over him. About half an hour afterwards Phillips and White fell heavily, and in a short time Phillips had to give up all idea of participating further in the contest, his example being followed by Markham after he had completed 78 miles.

"Just before five o'clock Stanton took some refreshment whilst riding and in throwing the vessel back to his attendant he swerved slightly, and Evans being close on him a collision occurred, both coming down heavily." And so it went on, alternating excitement and tedium.

The winner was Bill Cann, who came from the steel city of Sheffield. He had led ever since Phillips and Markham had abandoned and he finished with 1,060 miles. He had lost 7 lbs. His bike, little different from the one he would have ridden on the road, had a 52-inch gear, which meant each turn of the

Illustration of the first Six Day race at the Agricultural Hall, 1878. (source: *Penny Illustrated Press*)

pedals took him little more than half as far as a modern bike. The company that made it, Hydes and Wigfull of Sheffield, was so grateful that they gave him a job. The link between races, winners, and commercial interests was clear.

The attraction among those who wanted more than a two-wheeled version of bear-baiting wasn't Cann, though, much though he was billed as "Long-Distance Champion of the North." It was the Frenchman Charles Terront.

He worked each day when he wasn't racing as a bike-messenger for the Havas picture agency in France, which the British decided made him too much of a professional. The fact that they, too, were competing for money and could also have been bike-messengers or anything else seems not to have affected their argument. Better, Terront justified their prejudices of the "typical" Frenchman as bad-tempered, contrary and, of course, devious. And Terront did little to charm them out of it. He made no attempt to disguise that he was racing for money, openly demanding his prizes in cash.

They, of course, set out to undo him. Terront complained that the British riders all hated each other and that the only thing they could agree on was to gang up against him. That, he said, included arranging to be served their food in the saddle whereas he had to leave the hall for a café. Perhaps it is was due more to his own bad preparation, along with arriving late for the start, but coupled with the sickness he felt on the unbanked track, it did little to cheer him up.

It seems that at some stage the British riders offered a truce. They tried to befriend him, he said, by bringing him flowers which they repeatedly insisted he sniff. Far from the scent, he smelled a rat and decided they'd been sprinkled with a sleeping powder. From then on, he wouldn't accept anything from anyone, including food, and started to see his café trips as time-wasting but essential.

Not that Terront was above the odd ruse of his own. In February 1893, a promoter engaged him to ride an extraordinary 1,000 km race against another big-hitter of the day, Valentin Corre of Brittany, who had placed third in Bordeaux–Paris. The distance would have been remarkable enough, but the city of Paris made things harder by refusing to keep the lights on all night in the indoor track. The organizers had to borrow generators and lamps from workmen at a building site near the Eiffel Tower. They then borrowed braziers to warm the spectators, but they were pretty hopeless on February nights, and

those who stayed late ripped out 600 seats, set fire to them and warmed themselves round the bonfire.

The race took 41 hours and 2,500 laps of the Galérie des Machines, plus a
lot of liquid. Both men had to deal, as the French newspapers put it, with their
biological needs. Corre refused to give in to his bladder until he had seen that
Terront had been forced to. But even after 27 hours there was no sign that
Terront was in anything but perfect health. Finally Corre could stand it no
more, pulled into the track center, hid behind his assistants and felt the relief
that only a man who hasn't relieved himself for 27 hours can possibly feel.

Until then both men had been level. By the time Corre had remounted, he
was six laps down. Each lap was 800 m — the track was later rebuilt at 333 m
and with bankings — so he was close to two and half kilometers in arrears.
Hours later it happened again, Corre losing still more time, and still he could
not work out how Terront had done it. The reporters at the track had, though.
One of the papers next morning had the headline *Le coup de la chambre d'air* —
a phrase that doesn't translate easily until you realize that *coup* means what it
does in *coup d'état* or *coup de grace*, and that a *chambre d'air* is an inner tube.

Terront had worked out the problem and given one of his pacers a length
of inner tube that he'd knotted at one end. Come the time, he'd crowd his assistants around him, take the inner tube, stuff it into the leg of his shorts and
fill it as he rode. It was as difficult as it was crafty, since Terront had no freewheel and had to keep pedaling. The job done, he passed the tube back to his
pacer, who emptied it and kept it for next time.

The trick was the sensation of an otherwise dull race, since two men cir-
cling for nearly two days isn't the stuff of legend and excitement. Those who
hadn't bothered to be interested in the competition now wanted to see
Terront use his inner tube, see what Corre could come up with as a solution,
and crowds formed all down the street. The seats were all taken and those
who still wanted to get in were prepared to pay much more than the five-franc
value of the ticket. The promoters had no scruples about letting in many
more than the hall held safely, and the police had to be called in when the
flimsy upper balconies began filling ten deep and people started sitting in the
rafters. The more the police demanded spectators come down, the more the
insults fell on them from the safety of the roof and the more the promoters
smiled as they counted their cash.

The 1,000 km passed in 41:50:4, with Corre at 9.3 km. The crowd came on to the track to carry Terront in triumph. Corre, meanwhile, could see the joke despite his exhaustion and disappointment. "Terront didn't even beat me by a tire," he told journalists afterwards. "He won by an inner tube."

Terront became France's first bike hero, the first André Leducq ("a rider who was liked by women, whom he honored as frequently as his track contracts," a friend recalled), Jacques Anquetil, Bernard Hinault, or Laurent Jalabert. He won the pioneer race from Paris to Brest and back in 1891, a race so long — 1,198 km — that spreading out the road maps reveals not just the course but the outline of northwest France. Pierre Giffard, the newspaper editor who initiated it, said he wanted a race so long that it would "go to the end of the world and back." It was his little joke; it went to the region of Finistère, which translates as "end of the world."

"And how many stops do you envisage?" a colleague asked him.

"None."

The man looked at him, his mouth opening and closing like a goldfish's, until eventually he gasped: "You're crazy. Something will go horribly wrong and you'll be responsible. And you'll never find anyone to ride."

Giffard wasn't discouraged, and on 11 June 1891 he explained in *Le Petit Journal* that "I imagine a utilitarian type of race, raced by people using the same machine from end to end… as a means of transport, complete with lantern and luggage." It could be "of some interest for national defense," he added, an unfounded message which would warm Frenchmen after the Franco-Prussian war of 1870–71, in which Germany routed France and captured Napoleon. It had ended only with the siege of Paris and the loss to Germany of Alsace and a third of Lorraine.

Terront was impressed and told all his friends: "That's the one I'm going to win." He went to Spain to train, enjoying the weather and getting used to hills that would prepare him for the Brittany countryside. Somebody warned him of bandits who stretched rope across the road at night, jumped on cyclists, took their money and sometimes even their clothes before sending them on their way more or less naked.

Terront didn't believe them but took a revolver nevertheless. And sure enough two men appeared from the shadows when he was riding home one evening from Pamplona. The night was warm but he neither relished riding naked nor engaging in a gun fight. He challenged them in Oc, a language used in southern France and northern Spain, and they hesitated. He was about to pull his revolver when his friends turned back to find him and the men vanished. Terront survived to ride the world's longest road race.

His greatest rival was a slender man from Bordeaux, with a wide mustache like Terront's, called Jacques Jiel-Laval. In May he had been the best Frenchman in Bordeaux–Paris, the race which had been a victory for George Mills and the other British visitors. If Jiel-Laval was mad about that, he would have been even more furious that Terront had changed camps and helped pace the winners.

Laval, as cold and calculating as Terront was fiery, wanted revenge and he took on Frédéric de Civry as his chief pacer. The "de" suggests aristocratic connections and indeed he was a descendant of the Dukes of Brunswick.

There is some question about where de Civry was born — either in Paris or in Britain of French nationality — but it was only a short life. He was born in August 1861, which made him 29 for Paris–Brest–Paris, and he died two years after the race. Had he lived longer, he might have been nailed, literally, for the trick pulled on Terront to stop his winning. Because, mysteriously, Terront flatted repeatedly while Laval was ahead of him, but not after he had passed him...

Terront was backed by Michelin. The French company was testing its *pneus demontables*, air-filled tires that could be removed from the rim. "Riding on air

Jiel-Laval (with the bike), flanked by Frédéric de Civry (seated) and some other celebrities of the period, including Clément (to the right of Jiel-Laval).

is a marvelous sensation that will transform the future of cycling," Edouard Michelin had predicted, "provided we can make the tire removable." In September 1891 such things were exciting, certainly risky. Laval preferred the solid tires of his own backer, Dunlop. Nails certainly wouldn't bother him and they wouldn't embarrass Dunlop.

Paris–Brest–Paris left Giffard's offices in the rue Lafayette in Paris to a bugle call at dawn. Giffard led the peloton along the Champs Élysées to the real start in the Bois de Boulogne, to the west, then caught a train to move ahead of his race. He and others waved handkerchiefs from windows and shouted encouragement every time their train passed the riders. Among the 400 they looked for were Paul de Vivie, who campaigned for multiple gears under the name Vélocio (his memorial is on the col de la République outside St.-Étienne) and the future Tour de France organizer, Henri Desgrange. They

## Whatever Happened to… Paris–Brest–Paris?

THE world's longest single-stage race was held every 10 years until war interrupted the sequence after 1931. It restarted in 1948 but floundered as riders lost interest and busier roads made the event harder to run. It became a *faux* race every four years for fast amateurs and a survival course for everyone else.

Cheating is still known. The organizers, the Audax Club Parisien, said in 2000: "Our attention has been drawn to flagrant irregularities, certain riders not having hesitated to cover some kilometers by car. Good for them if they are satisfied with their P–B–P and they can look at themselves in the mirror."

Nail-scattering ran right through cycling's early years. The first four riders in the Bordeaux–Paris of 1902 — Léon Georget, Lucien Petit-Breton, César Garin, and Rudolphe Muller — were all disqualified for strewing tacks.

It emerged that they didn't do it, that spectators had been behind it. Nevertheless the race was given as a tie between Edouard Wattelier and Garin's brother, Maurice. For César Garin it was just the start of bad news; in 1904, he was disqualified for cheating in the Tour de France, as indeed was his brother Maurice.

looked but they didn't see. Like half the entrants, de Vivie and Desgrange didn't start. And there were no women, because they weren't allowed.

The first 50 km were cobbles and the rest unsurfaced and dusty. Most riders had tires that were clamped to the steel rims of their Cléments, Humbers, and Peugeots. One or two had Dunlop pneumatics. The Michelins on the bike of rider number five, C. Terront, were so revolutionary that they hadn't gone on sale yet, and Terront wasn't very confident about them.

He confessed: "I was so worried about a puncture in one of my pneumatics that each time I thought about the nail which at any time might stop me dead in my tracks, I felt re-energized and by going very fast I thought I might be able to delay the moment."

And then…

> Night had fallen. In the darkness, I became even more worried and I think I went even faster, hardly even looking at the road in front of me. It wasn't just my muscles driving my bicycle; my nerves also worked pretty hard and I directed all my energies into my riding. Suddenly, I felt my bicycle give way beneath me… a puncture! My back wheel had gone flat. Shivering with horror, I got off my bicycle and with the help of my pacers found a big, brand new nail in my tire. A brand new nail!
>
> We could see lights in the distance. It would be very hard to make a repair right there on the road. It could be better to ride into town, where we could perhaps do the repair much more quickly than out in the fields at night. There was already a huge crowd in the town square, but I was hardly in the right situation to pay attention to their applause. One of the employees of the Michelin company, who were traveling in front of me to help repair any problems I might be having, took the tire apart and made the repair, an operation that took him 40 minutes!

And well it might, since it involved slackening 17 bolts on a metal rim, a procedure Michelin had forecast would take "only" 15 minutes.

Terront sat at a table with his head in his hands, despairing at lost time. But misery provided insight. The leader was an hour ahead and, so far as he knew, hadn't flatted. Terront, on the other hand, had stopped three times. And the last time he found not just a nail but a brand new nail. Nails fell from countrymen's boots now and then, but surely not new ones… His suspicions hardened next morning when he flatted once more before Morlaix. And then again six kilometers further on.

> A post-office employee and another worker who was passing by took out my wheel and repaired it. I was pleased to note that they worked much more skillfully than the specialist sent to do the job. But it was still more time lost. I was absolutely furious when I set off again, thrashing my bicycle almost as if I wanted to break it.

The race wasn't even halfway through. Terront had led, been passed, led again, and was now 40 minutes behind. He was barely leaving Brest after 33 hours when "my pneumatic tire was softening noticeably. I got off. A pin was embedded in my back tire. I didn't want to lose any more time in repairing a tiny leak so I pumped it up again and started riding again, but the tire was soon flat again. I was desperate and asking myself why I was continuing with the ride."

Terront, winner of the first
Paris–Brest–Paris in 1891.

Then his pacer's tire went down and again a new nail caused the puncture. A hundred meters later, Terront too flatted. Now the connection was clear. "De Civry had arrived… a few hours before I did. Was this true? Because of a nail, even a brand-new one, should I give up the struggle? Absolutely not!" To which Andrew Ritchie says, "I assume the suggestion here is that Terront suspects de Civry had scattered the nails."

Terront and Jiel-Laval kept switching places, Jiel-Laval going faster but stopping for breaks, Terront riding for more than 71 hours without sleep. His tires stayed up whenever he rode ahead of Laval and de Civry, went down whenever he dropped behind. They were now on the last leg to Paris, and Terront couldn't take chances any longer. His helpers told him where Laval had stopped to sleep, and, there being no set course, Terront avoided the hotel where he knew Jiel-Laval's helpers would be watching out for him. His flat tires were over. Skullduggery had been overcome by thinking.

Suffering now from exhaustion and sleep deprivation, his face filthy and streaked red from repeated nosebleeds, he found a regiment of fans riding beside him.

"They shouted all the way from Ville d'Avray [the western suburb where the 1903 Tour finished] into Paris: 'Vive Terront! Vive Terront!' Finally I went through Suresnes and the Bois de Boulogne, and there I was at the beginning of the boulevard Maillot, at the end of which was the finish. I wanted to put on a good show at the finish and, crouching low over the handlebars, I sprinted as fast as I was still capable. The crowd [estimated at 10,000, at 6:25 AM] went mad with delight and closed in, running, behind me as I passed by, and finally I crossed the finish line!" The third man was 24 hours behind, and riders were still trailing in days later.

Two things came of all this. The first is that nails played an important part in bike racing for several decades more and, since this is where we started, Six Day races became faster and ever more hideous.

# 3. Fools on Wheels

Bill Cann and Charles Terront had no idea what they had started. I don't think Cann ever participated in another one, but Six Day races continued— and they became a temple of bad taste, excess, misery, and drugs.

Maybe it says something of American taste at the turn of the century that a race that made only a single column in the Islington Gazette should become a huge attraction once it crossed the Atlantic. It was the Barnum & Bailey of bike races, grotesques for all tastes, nothing more asked than the price of a ticket and an abandoning of standards. For a while, the League of American Wheelmen tried to keep control, fighting to keep the sport amateur — or at

## The World's First Six Day Race

London, November 1878

| | | |
|---|---|---|
| 1. | Bill Cann (Sheffield) 1,060½ miles; £100 | |
| 2. | C. R. Edlin (Leicester) 1,025 miles; £25 | |
| 3. | F. J. Lees (Sheffield) 952 miles; £15 | |
| 4. | T. Andrews (Birmingham) 928 miles; £10 | |
| 5. | Charles Terront (France) 900 miles; £10 | |
| 6. | H. Higham (Nottingham) 707 miles; £5 | |
| 7. | A. Evans (Portsmouth) 704 miles.; £5 | |
| DNF: | J. Keen (London) and David Stanton | |

least not too overtly professional, while trying to balance the conflicting interests of its dues-paying amateur membership and a sport that was rapidly becoming more professional.

The sport liked the idea of having fewer controls, though, and in 1893 along came the rival American Cycle Racing Association. Its views on sport versus showmanship can be pretty well guessed from its Cash Prize League, its links with the National Baseball League, and its plans to build bike tracks round 12 of the league's grounds, and from its inception never pretended to be anything but an professional organization.

It was all too much for the League of American Wheelmen, and it dwindled away until by 1900 it was no more than a pressure group for better roads. It went out of business in 1942, although it reemerged in 1965, went through a couple of name changes, and now does bicycling advocacy under the name League of American Bicyclists.

The cycling historian Jim McGurn says:

> Track racing reached new depths of corruption and foul play once the LAW had renounced control. Events were plagued by intimidation, pushing and the 'pocketing' of opponents, whereby riders penned in a competitor while their teammate slipped past (…) Some of the most degrading, but also the most popular, events in cycling were the Six Day races of the 1890s. The American versions were characterized by heavy betting, bad language and pick-pocketing. Fans drifted in and out during the daytime, numbers swelled in the evenings and fell off again after midnight. To encourage impromptu sprints some fans offered inducements by waving dollar bills from the trackside, as a dog might be offered a bone.

Organizers cashed in fast, and they would have run the races for longer than six days had it not been for pressure from the church. In the United States, the church was a force to reckon with. The League of American Wheelmen had even forbidden competition on the Sabbath. That attitude stretched to some riders as well, despite the corruption some of them may have been happy to practice for the rest of the week, and the world sprint champion Major Taylor refused to race on Sundays.

Organizers were so conscious of the pressure — or ashamed of the shabbiness of the events they were staging — that they hired bands to play hymns until midnight on Sunday. You could buy tickets to get in, sure — there was no rule against taking money, only against having fun — but pointedly there were hymns until the clock ticked past 12 midnight and six days of self-destruction could begin with Christian propriety.

Ned Reading from Nebraska rode 260 miles in 14 hours without getting off in the New York race in 1896; Charlie Miller covered 2,088 miles in one Six Day of 1897, sleeping only four and a half hours of the nine and three-quarters he spent off his bike. Bill Cann, it's worth remembering, won at Islington with "just" 1,060 miles. In many later events that wouldn't even have won a prize.

Riders became desperately tired. The *Brooklyn Daily Eagle* reported: "The wear and tear upon their nerves and their muscles, and the loss of sleep make them [peevish and fretful]. If their desires are not met with on the moment, they break forth with a stream of abuse. Nothing pleases them. These outbreaks do not trouble the trainers with experience, for they understand the condition the men are in." Not all spectators did. One, new to Six Day racing, asked why a rider crouched on his bike every lap. "Oh," said his friend, "he thinks there's a low bridge there."

Riders could become gibbering wrecks, wobbling, falling, climbing back on only to fall again a few hours later. Some were said to have become unbalanced for life, although claims are difficult to prove. Certainly the worse they

Madison Square Garden, the home of America's early Six Day races, was located at the corner of Madison and 26th Street, across from the park.

got, the longer the line became at the box office and the quicker the price of tickets doubled to a dollar. What folk wanted was terrible suffering and the misery of grotesque wrecks. They went home satisfied.

"More than 12,000 persons screamed and howled with the maddest enthusiasm as the end neared," reported the *Worcester Spy* of the New York Six Day in 1896. "It was a race until the very last hour. The end saw twelve human wrecks. Never did men finish a long-distance race so terribly exhausted. Some of them were raving lunatics."

Major Taylor, in his first pro race after never racing more than 75 miles or on a small track — New York was 10 laps to a mile, or 160 m — slept just one hour for every eight that he rode. That was more than most, but he still hallucinated that he was being chased by a knifeman. Others imagined their bikes were stuck to the track or that spectators were hurling stones at them. "There were reports of 'brain aberrations' (…) sometimes they dismounted, stood still and gaped cluelessly," says Jim McGurn.

You don't have to wonder too long to work out why. More than tiredness was involved. You couldn't sleep for just four and a half hours in six days as some riders were doing unless you resorted to chemical intervention, still less if you were riding a bike race on a tight and crowded track.

The reports were quite open: riders started on black coffee, moved on to peppermint, and then to cocaine. Trainers — who often fell by the trackside from exhaustion themselves — dropped it on riders' tongues or mixed it with

## Survival of Six-Day Racing

Six-day racing survived the Depression because the time demanded brainless entertainment. But innocence ended with the war. Annual Sixes in Boston finished in 1933, Detroit in 1936, Chicago in 1948. New York hung on until 1950. European tracks grew desolate, the night sessions a refuge for drunks, partygoers who had missed the bus, and a small number of dedicated fans. In 1967, the London race began an afternoons-and-evenings formula. Originally denied the right to call itself a six-day — it called itself just the London Six instead — its formula soon spread and is now the general style.

butter and rubbed it into their legs. Many used strychnine, a drug that increases tension in tired muscles provided you don't take too much of it (after which the effect becomes permanent, of course). Torchy Peden of Canada, who won 38 sixes, said he had become so used to strychnine that by the end of his career he was swallowing enough to kill a horse. Riders were also filled with brandy and treated with nitroglycerine to help their breathing.

John Hoberman, professor of Germanic studies at the University of Texas in Austin, and author of the critical book *Mortal Engines*, says: "The Six Day bicycle races of the 1890s were de facto experiments investigating the physiology of stress as well as the substances that might alleviate exhaustion. The advent of cycling as a mass recreational and competitive sport during the 1890s came at the end of a century that had seen many experiments designed to measure the effects of (sometimes fatal) stress on animals, and in this sense the Six Day riders were continuing the work of experimental physiologists who were interested in finding out just how much abuse the animal or human organism could take.

"It is, therefore, not surprising that when the pioneering French sports physician Philippe Tissié performed the first scientific doping experiments in 1894, his test subject was a racing cyclist whose performances could be timed and who could be primed with measured doses of alcohol or any other potential stimulant."

You can be sure the riders didn't put themselves through it for science. They did it for money. New York paid the Irish rider Teddy Hale $5,000 when he won in 1896. Imagine what that's worth today. In fact, ask Economic History Services. The answer is that it had the same buying power at the end of the 19th century as $104,857 does at the beginning of the 21st Century. Couple that with the lower expectations of the period — there was less to spend it on — and for a week's work on a bike, indoors out of the rain, it wasn't bad going for someone who would not have had much of a job otherwise. And there was more from personal appearances and follow-up races afterwards. It was worth finishing "like a ghost, his face as white as a corpse, his eyes no longer visible because they'd retreated into his skull."

Public outrage began to swell. *The New York Times* complained in 1897 that "An athletic contest in which participants go queer in their heads, and strain their powers until their faces become hideous with the tortures that rack them, is not sport. It is brutality. (…) Days and weeks of recuperation will be needed to put the [Madison Square] Garden racers in condition, and it is likely that some of them will never recover from the strain."

The next year, New York and Illinois limited races to 12 out of 24 hours. What lawyers wanted was riders who went to bed by midnight and stayed there until noon, or at least to have 12 hours' proper rest. They reckoned without the wiliness of organizers, though. Promoters realized that if they opened their races to teams of two rather than individuals, they could race in relay and each would be on the track for only half the time. Therefore both men would have 12 hours' rest a day, if only in intervals. Not exactly what the legal men had in mind, of course, but by the time Madison Square Garden started its new two-man race in 1899 it was too late.

Races got a lot faster and probably a great deal harder. They were still 24 hours, even if riders relayed each other much less than in modern events and as a result had longer breaks and even sleeps. Whereas Charlie Miller rode 2,088 miles in 1897, he and his partner won in 1899 with 2,745 miles.

WHAT PROFITETH IT?

Above: Bill Cann (seated) and Charles Terront (right), shown during their 1879–80 bicycle racing tour to the US with Barry Etherington, who had organized the tour and went on to become a major commercial manager and cycling event organizer.

Left: Critical cartoon illustration. (Source: *New York Herald*, 1897)

The Australian Alf Goullet with a good partner could manage 2,790 miles in the new style of racing. Sure that was 1,395 miles each, a lot less than Miller by himself in 1897 (although 335 miles more than Bill Cann in 1878, though Cann had achieved that on a high-wheel bicycle, whereas the later races were ridden on pneumatic-tired safety bicycles, which, though not inherently faster, were significantly more comfortable to ride, thus allowing higher speeds to be maintained over a protracted time period), but any bike rider will attest that increasing the speed produces a disproportionate rise in misery.

European promoters watched the change with interest. French promoters called them races "à l'américaine" or "American-style." In English the two-man tag race is still called a madison. But they adopted the new way only reluctantly. The southern French city of Toulouse was the first to try it in Europe, in 1906, but the event died on the third day when too few people thought it worth watching. The formula worked in Berlin three years later, though, and after that Brussels succeeded in 1912 and Paris in 1913. It's been the way things have been organized ever since.

Six Day races are exciting now, but during the heyday of the Madison Six Days, the hullabaloo among people of all sorts was colossal. Bing Crosby used to attend and song-pluggers would follow him as he walked to the track, singing songs in the hope he would like one. He apparently loved the crashes and was said to pay the hospital bills of injured riders. The actress Peggy Joyce would give $200 primes whenever the action struck her as flagging. She could afford it: Cole Porter once wrote a song that boasted "My string of Rolls Royce's is longer than Peggy Joyce's." Several bands could play at the same

Scenes from an 1897 Six Day race at Madison Square Garden. (Source: *New York Herald*, 1897)

time in the track center and she was so pleased when one spotted her and struck up Pretty Peggy with Eyes of Blue that she handed over a single prime of $1,000.

Organizers loved it when people put up primes. Why offer your own money when the public would do it for you? And this being cycling, it's no surprise that the idea came from a sleight of hand. The first primes were cash handed straight from spectators to individual riders, in the way that diners tip a waiter for good service — or as a bone to a dog, as Jim McGurn put it. The idea of milking the crowd for the general kitty came later, from an old French runner called Georges Berretrot.

Berretrot was the speaker, or announcer, at the main tracks in Paris. He knew that, even then, the crowds preferred to see road stars in their Sixes, even though few of them were much good on the track. The track specialists were fast and talented but the advent of the Tour de France in 1903 meant that the real stars, the legends, were the men who overcame enormous distances and appalling conditions to win the world's greatest race.

One of the disappointments at the Vélodrome d'Hiver in Paris was a man called Jean Brunier, who was born in the city in September 1896 and died only in January 1981. Brunier's record has disappeared, as has just which event it happened in, but he did little but crash, and the crowd began to think it had paid good money to see an incompetent. Berretrot realized the people were disillusioned and abandoned his microphone to follow Brunier into his cabin after yet another fall. There he found the unhappy rider tending to still more grazes from the steep wooden track.

Berretrot concocted a plot to change the crowd's mood... and to part it from still more of its money.

"Next time you crash," he told Brunier, "stick on the biggest bandage you can find, even if the injury's really minor."

Brunier looked puzzled.

"I'll whip up sympathy for you and we'll both profit." They agreed on a percentage of all that would be raised this way.

"D'accord!" Brunier laughed and he fell off another 15 times, often quite voluntarily. (Which, if you've ever tried it, you'll know isn't that easy — it suggests Brunier would have made a better trick cyclist than track cyclist.)

"Look at that poor courageous Brunier!" Berretrot appealed each time. "Let's help him. A little prime will help his suffering." The money rolled in.

From this you may assume that Six Day crowds were innocent at best and gullible in practice. Or maybe they saw through the ruse but admired its craftiness. Or maybe they were just drunk. Admirable behavior wasn't always their strength. The bad language and rowdiness that Jim McGurn said existed at the first Six Days in New York had less then entirely disappeared from the later events in Europe.

Ernest Hemingway lived in Paris between the wars, and in A Moveable Feast, published posthumously in 1964, he remembered the Vélodrome d'Hiver, or Vel' d'Hiv' for short — 250 meters round and lit by hanging lamps — for "the smoky light of the afternoon and the high-banked wooden track and the whirring sound the tires made on the wood as the riders passed." Others remember it still more colorfully.

So many people wanted to get in, that police had to put up barriers in the road to manage the crowd. The track was just a short walk from the Eiffel Tower and close to three Métro stations, so it was easy to reach. The richest took the best seats and the poorer, the late and those simply determined to have a good time regardless sat in the cheaper pesage (paddock) or balconies at the end of each banking. There they could see only two-thirds of the track but they did have the advantage of sitting above the people in the more expensive seats, on whose heads they could tip beer and half-eaten food. A good shot could even hit an official in the track center if he wandered too far from the judging area.

In 1932 they grew so angry when they thought the judges had penalized the wrong riders that they set fire to their newspapers and programs and threw them down on to the bankings, which must have concentrated the mind not only of the fire brigade and the builders of the wooden track, but the people over whose heads the flaming missiles were thrown.

The police were called and the race was neutralized. When it restarted it became clear that one of the riders, Henri Lemoine, had disappeared. Officials set off to search the building but returned to say there was no sign of him. Later it emerged that he had despaired of the whole business and gone back to his hotel to sleep.

Bottles rather than burning paper rained on to the track in 1935, and once more the race was halted when the judges put the local favorites Charles Pélissier and Antonin Magne a lap behind two Italians. A lap they had not lost.

Normally such things can be sorted out with a lot of shouting and whistling, but in this case there were other factors.

The first was that Charles Pélissier was the most glamorous of the three brothers, who dominated French road racing (his brother Henri was a better rider but a nasty piece of work, who was eventually murdered by his lover). Secondly, Italians were unpopular because Mussolini was conducting a brutal war in Ethiopia.

Pélissier got off his bike and confronted the judges, insisting — rightly — that he and the Italians were on the same lap. Getting no satisfaction, he walked off the track. Noticing what had happened, the crowd became still more incensed and started breaking up the chairs and throwing anything they could find. Pélissier, unmoved and probably impressed by the fuss, just sniffed "Why should I care if the fans are smashing the place up?"

He sat sulking in his dressing room for an hour before returning in tears. The other riders lined up to thank him when he came back, not only for making a stand against sloppy officialdom, but also because he had given them an hour's rest.

Six Day race at the Vél' d'Hiv', 1935. Six Day racing in Paris ended in 1959 and was not resumed until 1984, when the new track was opened in Paris-Bercy. (Source: AP)

Six Day riders upset at the frequent claims that the races are fixed make the not unreasonable response of "To fix it, you've still got to ride at 30 mph for an hour or more; if you can make it 35 mph, you can fix anything you like." Nevertheless, it's surprising how often the local star leads at the end of the first night, when there are still plenty of tickets to sell.

Although there may be disagreement over whether or not there are riders' combines now, there certainly have been in the past. It was at the Vel' d'Hiv' that the notorious "Blue Train" got started. The Paris Six had 15 or 16 teams, five of them big names and the rest on a lower level, although still popular. The Blue Train was named after a luxury express from Paris to the Mediterranean whose passengers were made up of society's big-rollers. It went fast and

## Shame of a Nation

The Vel' d'Hiv' died of its own shame. In 1942, Parisian policemen rounded up 12,000 Jews on behalf of the Nazis, often showing a great deal of enthusiasm themselves, and held them in the track with no working lavatories, and food and water supplied only by charities. They were then shipped to the Drancy concentration camp in a half-finished apartment block on the edge of the city. Some were reported to have thrown themselves from the bankings before the trains arrived. Most went from Drancy to Auschwitz, and fewer than 400 returned. They included none of the 4,501 children. Of the 9,000 policemen involved, only one resigned in disgust.

France refused to acknowledge for 40 years just how deeply its police force had been involved. Then, on 16 July 1995, president Jacques Chirac admitted "those black hours [that] tarnish our history and are an insult to our past and to our traditions. Yes, the criminal madness of the Occupiers was supported by the French, by the French state."

The track was pulled down in 1958 after a fire which some say was deliberate. It stood in the rue Nélaton, a short walk from the Eiffel Tower, but there is no sign of it now, except that the area outside Bir-Hakeim *Métro* station is named now after *la grande rafle du Vélodrome d'Hiver* — the great roundup of the Vel' d'Hiv'.

demanded a lot of money, and so did the stars on the boards of the Vél d'Hiv and elsewhere.

The combine began when the stars realized that it was them that the public were coming to see. The rest of the field were just cannon fodder. And so the established names who made up the informal Blue Train of élites demanded — and got — two thirds of the prizes. Automatically. However they rode, wherever they finished, two-thirds of the money would go to their one third of the field and the rest would scrabble for the remaining third.

(There is a modern echo of this, incidentally, in that all those sprint and miss-and-out prizes that riders seem so unenthusiastic about are shared out in proportion to where riders finish in the overall result; "How could it be otherwise?" says Phil Corley, a former Six Day minnow himself. "It'd be carnage if everyone went flat out for every penny.")

Fausto Coppi was in the Blue Train, and so were Hugo Koblet and Roger Rivière, and the Australians Sid Patterson and Russell Mockridge, and the Swiss sprinter Oskar Plattner. Not all rode at the same time, of course, and not all rode all the Six Days. But they had an automatic ticket for the Blue Train and nobody disputed their presence.

Stars and reputations are destined to be toppled, though. It didn't happen often, because Blue Train riders had influence away from the track as well, al-

This street name plaque is the only reminder of the Vél' d'Hiv' in Paris, marking the place where it once stood as the site of "la grande rafle du Vélodrome d'Hiver (the great roundup of the Vel' d'Hiv' — see box on preceding page).

most always influencing who got contracts in their road teams, sometimes dictating who would be allowed to ride criteriums alongside them, and now and then powerful enough to deny a Six Day contract to a rider who had upset them. Nevertheless things occasionally got so bad for lesser riders, upset with poor contract fees and prizes, that they squeaked loud enough to make their presence — and injustice — felt.

The Vél' d'Hiv' Six never stopped, even in the small hours. Normally the riders on the track ambled in tracksuits at night, reading or shaving, while the other half of the field dozed. But not always. Sometimes huge chases — jams — could start in the night as a minor team sought revenge. It happened one night at 6 AM, with barely a soul paying to watch. A huge battle broke out, with riders ducking, weaving and sprinting as if it were the final hour. Riders expecting a pleasant few hours in their beds were woken rudely and told to get dressed for battle.

The director, Louis Delblat, was beside himself with rage. "Make them stop, make them stop!" he screamed. "They'll be too exhausted when the public comes in." But the war raged on. Laps were taken and lost, reputations made and flattened, and the boards thundered. In the end, despairing, Delblat ran up the track and jumped over the wall into the stands. And there he lifted the seating and began hurling it on the track. Only then did the riders stop.

Sometimes bigger names had a go as well. It was speaker Berretrot's job to decide who would win the prize for each night's most popular rider. The favorite one year was a wisecracking man called Roger Hassenforder, who now runs a hotel near Colmar in eastern France.

## Feuding Merrily Along

The Blue Train may no longer exist, but it still doesn't pay to upset the order. The world's best six-day rider, the Dutchman Peter Post, rode the 1971 London six and collided with the American Jackie Simes on the opening night. The British rider Tony Gowland then ploughed into Post. The injury was more to pride than flesh but the row continued in the track centre and turned into a scuffle. Simes didn't ride another six that season, and soon afterwards returned to America.

"Hassen," as he was generally called, was the kind of bike rider you would like to spend more time with. Despairing of the tedium of a UCI banquet in Paris one night, he rounded up a dozen pigeons and set them loose all at once. The birds panicked and flew up to the roof and chandeliers and dislodged clouds of dust on to the startled diners. After the 1956 Tour de France, he took his celebration lap of the Parc des Princes seated on the handlebars and facing backwards. And his specialty in criteriums was to grab women's hats as he passed, a trick that went horribly wrong when he found out too late that a woman had fastened her bonnet beneath her chin.

Hassenforder didn't lack talent — he had "a Bobet in each leg," he boasted, referring to the triple Tour winner Louison Bobet — but he wasn't a big enough name to make the "Blue Train." Paris, like Antwerp, once had three-man teams, and one year he was teamed with two track specialists, Milo Carrera and Pierre Iacoponelli. He didn't have their speed, but he did have a roadman's popularity and rolling power. Convinced that he was the favorite of Berretrot and the crowd, he launched a lone attack that went on and on.

Oskar Plattner (known as "the sergeant-major" for his bossy manner) shouted at Carrera to make him stop, but Hassenforder took no notice. He rode harder and harder until, looking for Carrera and Iacoponelli to take over, he found both had slipped off the track and were sitting in their cabin.

Then the Blue Train retaliated. The great artillery of offended pride thundered at the poor fool who had started it all. Hassenforder, smashed, lost a few meters, then dozens of meters, and finally five laps. Dizzy with fatigue and disgusted at what had happened, he packed his bags and went home. As Carrera pointed out afterwards: "The Blue Train... I have to work with those guys all year. I'm not going to piss in the nest for *conneries* [damned stupidity] like that."

# 4. Men in Blazers

The men who run the sport are the officials of the UCI, the Union Cycliste Internationale, and they have been doing it for about a century now. Like most dignitaries, they probably take a dim view of having their grandeur reduced, and Hassenforder's pigeons would have been poorly received. But the organization that governs world cycling from its new headquarters in Switzerland — the "Chateau Verbruggen," as wags call it after its opinionated president, Hein Verbruggen — is in no position to complain about breaches of rules.

The UCI began as a French attempt to assert their authority over the British riders and organizers. The two nations have had a long history of antagonism, and the UCI is just another example.

The world's first cycling organization was set up by an English school teacher called Henry Sturmey. If you've ever ridden a three-speed hub gear, it was likely his name, and that of the engineer James Archer, that was engraved on it. Sturmey-Archer went on to dominate the world of enclosed hub gearing.

World cycling at the end of the 19th century was largely a European sport, and visiting Americans were as welcome, as colorful, but also as brief, as swallows in summer. English racing was administered by the NCU, or National Cyclists Union, which wanted an international organization so that there was some framework for its riders to race abroad and give foreigners a good seeing-to. Until then, there had been only so-called open championships run by

British promoters at the tracks they owned, notably in and around London, Birmingham, and Sheffield, plus occasional rival events in France.

The idea was the International Cycling Association, or ICA, and the NCU began writing to the world's other cycling bodies to ask what they thought about it. That was no quick task in an era with no international telephones and no radio links. Going abroad to meet foreign counterparts was also difficult, every border needing a visa and customs formalities, every nation a new language and no guarantee of admission. This was an era when foreigners, in most people's eyes, were people you went to war against. Nevertheless, the ICA got going in 1893, helped by "all the other cycling countries of the world" — being limited to those to whom the NCU fancied writing.

Despite, or perhaps because of all this, the little international gathering of the ICA got established, and started holding World Championships for both amateurs and professionals. The first was in Chicago in 1893. Not all were that successful, but they were heavily dominated by English-speaking riders in general and the British in particular.

In the end, the French objected, both to that and the way it alleged the ICA was powerless to solve international disputes. The British writer and official George Herbert Stancer summarized it as follows: "Objection was taken to Britain's alleged domination over international racing. This domination was more apparent than real, for the NCU exercised no control or influence over the independent governing bodies of Scotland, Ireland, Australia, South Africa and Canada." Wales hadn't joined in.

To an Englishman, there was nothing odd in this. But the French showed the confusion then that many have shown since over the difference between England (a single country vaguely akin to an American state), Britain (the three countries of the mainland: England, Scotland, and Wales), the United Kingdom (Britain plus Ireland, or these days just Northern Ireland), the British Isles (the UK and all the islands dotted about it, including the independent states of Ireland and the Isle of Man — just a geographical definition, therefore) and the British Empire, or Commonwealth (an association of independent states, including Canada and Australia, of which England, Scotland, Wales, and so on are simply equal partners).

To the French, though, all this was just a ruse to get the "English" extra teams. Once they had filled an English team, they complained, they just sent more but called them "Scotland" and so on. Worse, they called on riders from all over the world under the guise of the British Empire.

The first World Championships were held in Chicago in 1893 (where the American rider Arthur Zimmerman won the 1 mile sprint, and the South African Laurens Meintjes won the 100 km race). In the next years, World Championships were held in Antwerp (1894), Cologne (1895), Copenhagen (1896), Glasgow (1897, where English motor-paced riders won all the medals in the professional 100 km event and the gold medal in the amateur 100 km), Vienna (1898), and Montreal (1899). Then came Paris in 1900.

As usual, the competing nations sent officials to a pre-championship meeting, to talk about the way things would be run. And there France insisted that "England" send only one team. What's more, "England" would also represent the British Empire, which by that time included much of the world.

The British were aghast. There had been nothing on the agenda, not a whisper of what was about to happen. "The British Empire in those days was much more of a political unit than the British Commonwealth of the present time," Stancer recalled, "but the governing bodies of cycling in each of the countries were independent enough." And Sturmey felt that they ought not to be kicked out in their absence.

"Gentlemen," he protested, a stickler for good procedure. "This is an outrage. I must insist we adjourn the meeting so that those who are not with us can be asked their views."

The meeting agreed another date, and the championships went ahead. Stancer set about his campaign to keep things as they were, but once more the French tripped him up. They called another meeting in Paris on April 15, earlier than the agreed date, to set up a new world cycling body, the Union Cycliste Internationale. It was just the International Cycling Association under a different name, with the stipulation that Britain was welcome to join — but as a single member and not in its separate parts.

It left Stancer no time to gather breath and the UCI got started without Britain, the country which had sought to formalize international bike-racing in the first place. It had been kicked out of its own club. The United States, Italy, Switzerland, and of course France joined at once, and Holland and Germany a couple of months later. That was more or less the end of the ICA, by now close to the *Marie Celeste* of cycling, crewed as it was only by Britain. And British riders themselves, caring more for bike racing than cycling politics, affiliated themselves to the UCI through their own body, the Professional Cyclists Union. But Britain itself was out in the cold.

Britain joined the UCI after its year of hurt pride and had the last laugh when it kept the separate votes for England, Ireland, Scotland, and Wales that had caused the split in the first place, and when its riders proved to be a major force in UCI championships, just as they had been in the old ICA.

The UCI's troubles never went away, though, and to this day there are rebel — or at least unallied — national bodies in almost every country in the world, happy to put on bike races and even championships outside the UCI.

Not all World Championships were successful, especially at first. Take the first professional championships, held in Cologne in 1895, for instance. The big event was the sprint, in which Robert Protin of Belgium was riding against George Banker, the son of an American tycoon, and Huet, another Belgian. Protin, a man with a little mustache, lined up closest to the starter. There was a lot of tension and everyone was nervous, not least the starter because he brought down the starting flag and poked it in Protin's eye.

Protin, predictably, didn't win. Instead, he was rubbing his watering eye and complaining as Banker set about his victory lap. Judges, managers and

Robert Protin, who won the 1895 World title under questionable circumstances over the American rider George Banker in Paris.

anyone else who cared to join in went into a huddle and eventually the riders were told to ride again.

"I won't," said Banker.

"You will," retorted the judges.

"I won't," said Banker.

"Then you won't be World Champion," said the judges, and so Banker got up again and this time the now bloodshot Protin became World Champion. Banker was anything but a good loser and, stuck for any more convincing reason, complained that he had been demoralized. He must have been convincing because he started getting support. The ICA fretted for weeks. Then it said both races would be canceled and there would be another, only to face opposition from another direction.

"You do that," said the Belgians, "and we'll leave the ICA."

That was more than the ICA could face, and it despaired of the whole thing and said Protin could stay World Champion and that was the end of it. He died in Liège in 1953 at 82. He had been national champion in 1891, 1892, 1893, and 1894, won the national 100 km title in 1893, the European sprint championship in 1892 and 1893, the French open 5 km championship in 1893, and taken the world 500 m record in 1895. You can't help thinking the guy deserved to win the world title.

But then what of Willie Falk Hansen and Lucien Michard? They were riding the World Championship sprint in Denmark in 1931. Hansen was the local man and Michard the Frenchman who had won the previous four years. In their case there were just two men in the final, and the judge, Albert Colignon, watched them circle the track, noted who was on the left and who on the right as they reached the last 200 meters, and then concentrated on the line. He had no trouble judging that the inside wheels crossed it first and announced Hansen as World Champion.

Except that he wasn't. Even the Danish crowd, which would have loved to see Hansen win, could see he'd been clearly beaten. Horrified, Colignon realized that the two had changed sides in the last 200 meters, the rider on the left now being on the right as they crossed the line. It was Michard he'd seen and not Hansen. It was an epic mistake, but understandable, and he was happy to acknowledge his error.

However…, the UCI in those days insisted that a judge's result, once announced, couldn't be changed. Even if it was wrong; even if the judge *knew* it was wrong. Colignon had named Hansen World Champion and that was that. The runner-up was the winner. Hansen got his rainbow jersey and wore it for the rest of the year. And Michard? He made himself a champion's jersey of his own design and the pair cleaned up for the rest of the season in grudge matches all over Europe.

It wasn't the happiest championship...

The road race in 1931, unusually, was a time-trial. Above all, that pleased the British. They had abandoned massed-start racing on the roads at the end of the 19th century because of police harassment. Although opposition was quite widespread and there is a long history of conflicts with other road users, the most quoted incident that is thought to have triggered the law was that of a woman driving a carriage, who had panicked as a group of riders passed her 60 miles north of London and her horse pushed three of the riders into a ditch, where their bikes were wrecked. The woman complained to the police, Britain feared for the future of all cyclists on the road — their position had been repeatedly threatened by legislation — and races from then on were held as time trials at dawn, in out-of-the-way places, the venues kept secret even in

## Britain and the UCI

Britain almost managed to be thrown out of the UCI twice. Fifty-six years after the debacle of 1900, the UCI told it that unless it sorted out the civil war between the NCU and the newer British League of Racing Cyclists over whether there would or would not be mass-start racing on public roads, the cycling world would accept world championship teams from neither.

Stancer protested that the NCU was older than the UCI "and possessing a better record of integrity" and deserved more respect. "There is nothing new in the idea of dictatorship in international cycling sport, or the disregard of constitutional practice. If there is anything in hereditary tendencies, the UCI could hardly have been expected to act otherwise," he said.

In the end, the NCU and the BLRC fought themselves close to bankruptcy and, financially and mentally exhausted, merged to form the British Cycling Federation.

cycling newspapers. Riders dressed from neck to ankle in black for "obscurity" and carefully made sure they had bells to stress their law-abiding nature. Certainly there were no race numbers.

Emergency measures have a habit of hanging on, though, and Britain was still stuck with that rule when it ran the World Championships in 1922. Hindsight shows there was nothing to fear from the sort of racing popular on the European mainland, but that wasn't the view at the time. And signs of decades of isolation from mainstream racing showed so badly that the races were taken away before they'd ended and moved to Paris.

The track events were run at New Brighton, across the river Mersey from Liverpool. The circuit was 586 yards long and dated from 1898, when the surface of badly matched cement and gravel must have seemed perfectly acceptable. By 1922, though, Continental tracks were being built to much higher standards, and visiting riders were openly contemptuous of where they were being asked to ride. Worse was that the track became treacherous in the rain — and Liverpool is one of the wettest cities in England.

The sprinter Piet Moeskops "attempted a trial spin but his machine slipped on the greasy surface and he returned limping slightly and shaking his head," the *Wallasey and Wirral Chronicle* reported. He never rode at New Brighton again, the professional sprint race having been moved to Paris before he got the chance. The motor-paced events weren't even attempted, so dangerous was the track.

Britain not only had difficulty running the World Championship, but the British weren't even much interested in watching. There was room in the new stand for crowds far exceeding the actual attendance, which never exceeded 8,000. The organizers — the Anfield Bicycle Club in Liverpool and the local section of the NCU — found so little interest among local companies that it had to advertise in local papers for people willing to advertise in the championship program.

Even giving people their money back couldn't be done properly. The lines for people seeking refunds for expensive seats were filled enthusiastically by those who had held cheaper seats and had found to their delight that they were not being asked for proof.

"The management of the meeting left much to be desired," said the *Wallasey and Wirral Chronicle*.

The one event that did go off well was the one that least appealed to the visiting nations — the road race. Britain still believed that road racing would bring police wrath and the end of all cycling, so the championship was run as a 100-mile time-trial in the Shropshire area of central England. The British couldn't insist that foreign riders join the British in wearing their normally compulsory black-sleeved jackets and full-length tights but they certainly made their own team do so.

The foreigners' smirks ended, though, when British riders, to whom riding 100 miles unpaced was a normal event, took the first three places. It confirmed the smug British view that only racing alone against the clock produced true champions. Gold, silver, and bronze proved both that and the athletic superiority of the winners.

They were thrilled when Denmark saw things the same way in 1931. Britain sent Freddy Frost, Len Cave, and Frank Southall, with F. T. Brown (initials were common in those days) as reserve.

*Cycling* triumphed: "The world's amateur road race championship is absurdly simple this year... It is, therefore, perfectly easy to jot down the English times, note the best times abroad over the distance, and announce the result long before the starter has given the Danish equivalent for the word 'go'!"

There was some irony, but the headline still read: "If Perfectly Fit Southall Will Win The World's Road Championship, predicts 'The Loiterer.'"

"The Loiterer" was disappointed. The race was a disaster. The police did not close the roads and anybody could follow the riders. Faster competitors ran into the convoys following slower ones, and Southall, like others, freely ac-

## Whatever Happened to… the Grand Prix des Nations?

The fiasco of the 1931 world championships did have a happy outcome. The professional race, won by Learco "The Locomotive" Guerra of Italy, thoroughly impressed the French newspaper editor Gaston Bénac and his star writer, Albert Baker d'Isy. There were few time-trials in those days, and none at all in the Tour de France until 1934. They went back to *Paris-Soir*, their evening paper, and founded the Grand Prix des Nations. It was the virtual time-trial championship of the world until the UCI established a formal one six decades later.

cepted he had sat on a wheel for 20 miles. "The whole race was as badly orga-nized as a road time-trial could be and was a disgrace," sniffed *Cycling*'s editor.

Crowds massed round the timekeeper, who couldn't see the riders. Num-bers were called in one language and translated into others before they reached him. He missed Southall completely, but the British timed him at 5:6:26. The timekeeper left off the seconds and logged him at 5:6. At least five others got the wrong times, and it was anybody's guess who had done what. Southall ended up as 5:6:30, which sounds little better than a guess. The writer for *Cycling* reported:

A time was recorded against a competitor's number given as 53. About that moment I had myself observed a rider crossing the line carrying the number 66 (Olmo, Italy). Three-quarters of an hour later an Italian delegate ap-proached the timekeeper's table and for some moments completely monopo-lised the attention of the officials whilst he claimed that Olmo had arrived and that he had crossed the line "one second after Henry Hansen." After some minutes of heated discussion in French, Italian, Danish (and I could not resist saying a word, too), the time previously recorded against 53 was transferred to 66 and Olmo was listed second in the Amateur Road Championship of the world.

The next sentence is plaintive:

What happened to No. 53, T. Wanzenried, of Switzerland, I cannot say. He is not shown on the finishing list at all.

This is how things looked as individual riders (here the German rider Erich Metze) started for the 1931 World Championship road race time trial. (Source: Gronen & Lemke)

And would you like another, more recent, example of confusion? How about Paris–Roubaix in 1949?

Imagine yourself in the crowd. All afternoon loudspeakers have been telling you of the drama on the road, that the leaders were on the city outskirts, that they were approaching the track, that they were about to make their glorious and muddy entrance. You lean forward like everyone else, you stand for a better view. You gasp with excitement and a roar goes up around the stadium. And then…

And then, as you stare at the empty hole of the tunnel leading from the outside, there's a disturbance and you turn your eyes and, stunned, you see the leaders clambering down the press stand and on to the track. No race has ever finished in greater chaos.

To this day the Paris–Roubaix of 1949 has two winners. They finished separately, four riders apart and by different routes… and it took two international conferences to sort them out.

What happened was that three riders had reached the track together. Then an official sent them down a side-road. André Mahe, Jacques Moujica, and

## The Tax Man Cometh

Perhaps Paris–Roubaix is more prone to cock-ups than other races. Certainly it started earlier. The 1907 winner was a Frenchman born in London, Georges Passerieu. He rode for Peugeot, which had sent its riders over the course before the race and decided that Passerieu, a poor sprinter, should go for a lone win. And that's just what he did. He got to Douai with a group of favorites and outjumped them, holding his lead to Roubaix. He looked in desperate happiness at the track gates ahead of him. He had only to ride through them, turn right, ride a lap… and win.

Instead, a policeman stepped into the road, his hand turned flat into Passerieu's face. He was to stop. The policeman had waited for hours to check that Passerieu had paid his bicycle tax.

Happily, the tax plate was in order, the policeman was satisfied, and Passerieu won Paris–Roubaix, although he was only just crossing the line when the second man arrived.

Frans Leenen looked for somewhere to go. Moujica turned a tight circle, fell off and broke his pedal. Mahe and Leenen rode round the track looking for a way in and discovered the door to the press seats. And that was how they got to the banking, climbing back on their bikes and sprinting for the line.

The judge, Henri Boudard, sent Mahe on his lap of honor. But unfortunately for him, the bunch sprint a few moments later was led by Serse Coppi, who protested that he was the winner. Novel though climbing down the press seats was, it wasn't part of the course and the two should be disqualified or demoted. Strange echoes of Arthur Linton's win in Bordeaux–Paris in 1896...

Mahe was in the shower when he got the news. The judges had sided with Coppi.

"I only followed the rules," Boudard moaned.

The organizers gave Mahe and the others their prizes anyway, and five days later the French federation confirmed Mahe as the winner. "It couldn't be otherwise," said Achille Joinard, the federation president.

"It certainly can!" said the Italians, and they appealed to the UCI. Now it was an international row. The race had been in April. In August the UCI decided to annul the results, although it could not think what to do next and said it would meet again in November. Now neither side was happy. Belgium sided with Italy and Joinard was called a traitor for soft-pedaling the French cause in trying to become UCI president. That gave the scandal a fresh spin, and in November the UCI said both riders could have it.

"Thank heavens there's another Paris–Roubaix in four months," said one official.

If you ever organize an event, however humble, or accept a job on a committee however minor, remember the ICA, the UCI, Robert Protin, Willie Falk Hansen, Paris–Roubaix, and the World Championships of 1922 and 1931. And reflect on how gloriously things can go wrong, when they get the chance.

# 5. Simply Cheating

Doping apart, do bicycle racers cheat more than participants in other sports? Perhaps they do. Perhaps they just get more chances. You can't take a shortcut in the 100 meters dash. And while there was an entertaining period in 1977 and 1978 when swimmers were reported to have begun pumping air up their backsides to make them float better, there's not much you can do in a swimming pool either.

Cycling, on the other hand, goes on for hours on empty roads with riders separated into groups or individuals which judges can never hope to supervise. That was never more the case than in the old days, when races went through the night and riders could be separated by hours.

There was so much cheating in the second Tour, in 1904, that Henri Desgrange swore he'd never run another. Riders rode behind cars or even inside them. If officials were too close by, the trick was to tie a thin wire to a door handle and bite on a cork tied to the other. You could still pedal, the grimace of biting gave the impression of effort, and you could close gaps or bowl along with satisfying ease.

Spectators joined in, too. They let their favorites pass and then felled trees across the road in the darkness to hold up the chasers. On the Col de la République outside St.-Étienne they went still further and simply beat up riders they didn't want to win. The traveling organizer, Géo Lefèvre, had to fire his gun to disperse them.

I rode over the Col de la République a while back, and I could still sense the atmosphere at what is now a parking area next to a monument to Paul de

Vivie. It's no longer a bleak place as it must have been then, but you only have to wait for a gap in the passing cars and then half-close your eyes to imagine the shouting, the sound of blows, the gunshots, and the rattle of fleeing boots…

Outside Lyon, a driver repeatedly tried to force Maurice Garin and Lucien Pothier into a ditch to stop their beating more favored competitors. Henri Cornet, the eventual winner after the disqualifications that made the race a farce, claimed he had been fed chicken spliced with sleeping powder. Even more bizarre, Jean-Baptiste Dortignacq said rivals had put itching powder under his jersey. Louis Trousselier was accused of smashing the ink stands at the roadside controls so that riders behind him wouldn't be able to sign in.

In an echo of Charles Terront and Paris–Brest–Paris, both riders and spectators scattered nails on the road. Angry officials were reported to have swept up no less than 125 kg of nails on the first stage in 1905, from Meau to Châlon-sur-Marne. Only one rider didn't puncture, and just 15 of the 60 starters reached the finish by bike. Others arrived by car or train and it took a strike by riders to persuade Desgrange to let them stay in the race.

Nail-scattering was so widespread — sometimes by riders, sometimes by fans, sometimes by manufacturers who wanted to prove their tires could easily be repaired, and at times by people who simply didn't want their lives disturbed by having the Tour de France ride by — that an inventor called Cavalade took advantage of the rest day at Toulouse to demonstrate a puncture-proof tire in the Café Sion. A reporter wrote: "Dortignacq got on the inventor's bicycle, rode quickly, then slowly, jumped on the pedals, balanced on the nails and jumped the bike on to them. There was no puncture, the nails falling from the tires at the first turn (…) All the Tour riders tried it (…) The bike was convincing and the riders warmly thanked M. Cavalade, who put the invention at their disposition, without obligation, for the stages still to come."

There has been more immediate sabotage. Paul Duboc, a 27-year-old former carpenter from Rouen, had come 11th in the 1908 Tour and fourth in 1909, but was riding still better in 1911, when he won the stage into Perpignan and broke clear on the Portet d'Aspet next day on the first stage in the Pyrénées. That put him within striking distance of the leader, Gustave Garrigou. The race was on points rather than time and Duboc could make up the seven points he needed on the next stage, across the Peyresourde, Aspin, Tourmalet, and Aubisque on the way to Bayonne.

He attacked immediately the stage started at 3:30 AM. He led by 10 minutes over the Tourmalet, and rode on to the Aubisque. And there he wobbled and fell in front of a car which only just missed him. Racked by pain, he began writhing with vomiting and diarrhea. He lay there for an hour and a quarter, riders passing all the time, but the harsh rules insisted that any help would disqualify him.

Finally his manager, Paul Ruinart, gave him an emetic to clear his stomach. Duboc climbed back on his bike, still groggy, and began zigzagging to and from the open drop. Heroically, he still finished 21st, 3 hours 47 min. behind Garrigou.

Things like that don't just happen, of course. Rumors of poisoning began instantly. Garrigou was the obvious culprit because he had most to gain. Angry crowds threatened him as the race passed. They got angrier and angrier as the Tour approached Duboc's home town of Rouen, and Desgrange provided Garrigou with a bodyguard. That might have been enough had someone not pinned up roadside notices saying "Citizens of Rouen, I would be leading the race if I hadn't been poisoned. You know what you have to do when the race crosses the city." They were signed in Duboc's name.

The truth was that Duboc had nothing to do with the posters, nor had Garrigou anything to do with the poisoning. In fact he and Duboc — who had recovered quickly — were eating at neighboring tables in La Rochelle when they first heard of the threats. Duboc offered to go ahead and meet the people of Rouen and explain Garrigou's innocence. But Desgrange hit on another idea and disguised Garrigou with a mustache, new vest and different goggles. He begged the other riders to crowd round Garrigou as they rode and to stay together until after Rouen. They cooperated, the mob looked for Garrigou but failed, and there were fights when thugs realized they had been fooled. But it was too late. Garrigou won the Tour and Duboc came second, 18 points down.

That left the obvious question: who did it? The truth is that to this day nobody knows. There had been a control point in Argèles, a town between the Tourmalet and Aubisque, and Duboc remembered taking a bottle from happy spectators who were chanting his name as he signed the control book. He could have taken it from anyone — but someone must have arranged it. Years later there was said to have been a confession from François Lafourçade, coincidentally the first Tour rider to have crossed the Tourmalet and a man with a reputation for so-called wonder-drinks. He was banned for life but the details have never been published. We shall never know why he did it or how.

Garrigou himself became the victim in 1910. He recalled: "We were crossing Nîmes–Perpignan for the eighth stage. I took care the previous night, as always, to take my Alcyon cycle up into my room at Nîmes. It might have seemed a needless precaution because our team had so far dominated the Tour. The only scuffling for places was between ourselves. Anyway, I forgot to lock my door, a mistake which cost me dearly.

"We were going through Lunel at about 3 AM, when my front wheel gave up, ball bearings spilling everywhere. Someone had done a good job of unfixing the hub, and I hadn't noticed a thing. So I had to find a mechanic — at 3 AM — and then search for bearings of the right size to replace those I had lost. I lost an hour and a half of that. And I had been within seconds of (my big rival) François Faber."

You may by now be wondering about the control points. What you have to remember is that the rules of the game were constantly evolving and were adapted to changing circumstances. The first races were trials of attrition, marathons in which the fastest runner sets the pace and the rest match him or trail in hours later. The roads weren't closed. They didn't need to be, because there was no traffic — and there were no marshals or motorcycle outriders. The few cars available to carry officials were notoriously unreliable — Desgrange was once reduced to chasing his own race in a horse-drawn cart — and at first the stage towns were decided according to which towns judges could reach by train.

The organizing newspaper, *L'Auto*, did have representatives dotted about France, however, and they and Tour officials cooperated in running control points. Riders were given route sheets and told to sign control sheets at intervals to prove they had gone the right way. As in modern *randonnées* or brevet rides, which are a direct inheritance of the control-sheet system, the checks were arranged wherever possible to make shortcuts impossible. But officials could not account for the improbable or the purely absurd. And so it was in 1922 that Émile Masson Sr., of Belgium, inadvertently finished three and a quarter hours behind Jean Alavoine on the Bayonne–Luchon stage. It had do with the wages of sin, explained his son, Émile Masson Jr.

"That day," his father told him, "I was flying. I dropped everyone on the first slopes of the Aubisque. I knew it would be cold and so I was wearing a thick flannel vest under my jersey. After a few kilometers I was suffocating. I felt like a fish on hot sand. I longed to stop. Three punctures on the descent gave me Philippe Thys as companion. He said he had food poisoning. We decided to eat at one of the restaurants in Bagnères-de-Bigorre. No sooner said than done. As we were leaving the place, Jacquinot and Bellenger turned up to eat. We waited for them and when they'd finished we set off together towards Ste-Marie-de-Campan, where they decided to abandon.

"Philippe and I resolved to press on. With mixed results. On the way up the Peyresourde, a shepherd suggested we take a shortcut on a goat track that went up the side of the mountain. The only solution was to carry our bikes. The stones were slipping beneath our feet and horseflies were biting our legs. We were getting nowhere. Rather than gaining time, we were losing it."

Despite all that, Masson finished 12th in Paris.

Others went beyond merely taking a shortcut. In 1906, Maurice Carrère, Henri Gauban, and Gaston Tuvache caught a train to Dijon, only to run into Tour officials who happened to be studying a map at the station exit.

In 1928, Francis Bouillet and Arsène Alancourt were dropped by the peloton and hitched a lift. A truck stopped for them only to skid and fall into a gulch a little later. With the happiness of chance, they climbed out and hailed a passing taxi, insisting their manager would pay the fare once they got to the finish. The odd thing is that they weren't disqualified. In those days riders could drop out of one stage and join in again later, although not for the overall prizes. Bouillet started again three days later.

Others were shrewder. The Frenchman Henri Alavoine used to delight in Desgrange's prickly nature and engage him in lengthy debates about the rules. Both men would grow ever angrier, and Desgrange was so busy gesticulating and debating, that he didn't notice Alavoine was clinging to his car and getting a free ride up a climb.

This kind of thing is not merely reported from the "pioneering days" of the sport, incidentally. Dutch riders were caught in mid-ruse at the end of the 1990s when officials noticed they had tied their feeding bags to the side mirror of their team car and were getting a lift up the hill. The straps had been too thin to be seen from following cars, but that year *commissaires* had started checking the race from a helicopter… Was it new? No: the 1933 winner and World Champion, Georges Speicher, was disqualified in 1938 for hanging on to a car…, just as Jacky Durand was in 2002. And as Roger Lapébie had perfected years earlier…

Roger Lapébie, brother of Guy, whom we'll meet again in the next chapter, was never a pleasant man, nor much concerned about the rules. He was warming up at Luchon in 1937, when he spotted that someone had sawn halfway through his handlebars.

The Tour had been won in two successive years — 1935 and 1936 respectively — by Romain Maes and Sylvère Maes, two unrelated Belgians. It is the only time the Tour has been won by riders of the same name. France had won for five years in succession before Romain Maes in 1935, and hadn't taken the upset lightly. Another Belgian win the following summer hardly made the mood better.

Relations between the nations in 1937 were sour from the start, both insisting the other was cheating. Belgium insisted it had been given severe penalties for petty offenses, while Lapébie was getting away lightly. The crunch came when Maes punctured and Gustave Deloor stopped to help him. Deloor was Belgian, but riding as an individual and not as part of the Belgian team, so Maes was penalized 15 seconds for accepting help from a rival (against the rules in those days) and Deloor 60 seconds for helping one.

Lapébie saw the pair halt and attacked. Maes and Deloor got within 75 meters of them when a railroad crossing closed in front of them. They were sure the signalman had done it deliberately, pushed their bikes under the barrier, crossed the tracks and started again. That upset French fans, and they pushed and jostled Maes when he got to Bordeaux. He and his team returned home, and the Belgian cycling association paid them the prizes they had missed.

In the middle of all this, it was no surprise that Lapébie — himself not beyond accepting illegal help in the mountains — considered that it must have been the Belgians who had sawn through his handlebars.

"They were staying in the same hotel," he said. "I put on new bars, but they had no bottle cage. [Riders carried drinks there rather than on their frame, frame cages being introduced only years later by René Vietto.] I was penalized every time someone handed a bottle up. I lost five minutes on the Tourmalet and panicked. I wanted to stop."

He was repeatedly warned for being pushed by spectators.

"I said, 'I can't stop the crowds pushing me. I'm asking them not to.' In fact, I was quietly asking them to push me harder." Belgian riders had already claimed that he had held on to a car in the Alps. They were right; Lapébie made up seven and a half minutes on the Peyresourde, Aspin, Tourmalet, and Aubisque in the Pyrénées by grabbing at cars and then riding behind French journalists. Desgrange, for whom the circulation of *L'Auto* depended on a French win, penalized him only a minute and a half. And that's what started the Franco–Belgian war in bicycle racing.

# 6. And Still More Cheating

Guy Lapébie took a long while to realize that he had been out-cheated in the 1936 Olympic road race, at the Berlin Games. He was leading a group of 50 in the sprint for the line when he felt his power going in the last 30 meters. His French teammate Robert Charpentier came by him and at the same time Lapébie realized why he had started weakening.

"When Charpentier attacked, I wanted to go with him," Lapébie said, "and to attack him. But a hand, I don't know whose, had grabbed my bike by the saddle. I had to reach behind me and bang it away." The result was Charpentier took the gold and Lapébie took the silver — the chocolate medallion, as the French call it — a bike's length behind.

Wlodzimierz Golebiewski, vice-president of the International Amateur Cycling Federation, completed the story: "Several months later, back in France, Lapébie was looking at a photograph of the finish… It was then, and in fact not until then, that he began to understand why he had suddenly slowed down… it was because his teammate Charpentier had caught hold of his shorts from the back."

In fact it wasn't a photo but a film, the work of the documentary-maker Leni Riefenstahl. Lapébie watched *Les Dieux du Stade*, as her two-part *Olympiad* was known in France, with great interest. It didn't matter to him whether it portrayed the Berlin Games as the struggle of athletes to go faster, higher, and further or as propaganda for the ideals of the Nazi dream. All he wanted to see was the bike race.

With some irony, *L'Auto* observed that "the last three kilometers of the race were particularly well filmed; you could see quite distinctly that Guy Lapébie was twice tugged back in the sprint, including once by Robert Charpentier."

A good tug of something — anything that comes to hand — is always good for a mass sprint. I know an old pro, Geoff Wiles, who has a picture of a race finish hanging in his bike shop. I hadn't seen him for years, since about the time the picture was taken, and he ran his picture over the glass surface of the frame for me and identified the faces one by one, men who had seemed impressively mature at the time but looked worryingly young now that I took a closer look at them, a few decades older myself.

"Now look more closely," he said, and I pressed my nose a little nearer. "See there, and there?" I looked as asked and then saw things that clearly the judges had never seen. "There's a hand tugging a jersey there, see? And there's another one. And there's someone leaning on someone else, and here's an elbow tucked round someone else's…" And so it went on. That's why he had it on the wall. It was a one-shot encyclopedia of how to grab and grapple in a mass sprint.

Geoff probably told me which race it was. I can't remember. It could have been just another Sunday afternoon race of no importance except to those who stood to win some prizes. In an Olympic road race, of course, it's different. In the Tour de France as well, you'd think…

The 1930 Tour turned out a battle between France and Italy, and in particular between the sprinters Charles Pélissier and André Leducq on the French side and Alfredo Binda and Learco Guerra on the Italian side. The bunch, when it got to the track at Bordeaux, would have been larger had it not been for a crash in the rain. Even so, about 60 riders hurtled on to the bankings together. Tracks are narrow, bunches of sprinters are nervous and hectic. And with the rivalry that had grown through the race, it was inevitable that something would happen.

"Four hundred metres before the banner, I got on to Leducq's wheel, because he was starting to sprint," Pélissier said. "Then I came off his wheel to cross the line in front of Aerts and Binda." Pélissier won. But Italian reporters who were watching were convinced they had seen rather more.

"He tugged Alfredo's jersey," they protested. And Binda soon insisted they were right.

"I attacked Pélissier about 120 metres before the line," he said. "When I came up alongside him, he grabbed my jersey, then he put his hand on my shoulder to throw himself towards the line. I've never known anything like it and I'm going to quit."

The officials agreed, and Pélissier was demoted and Jean Aerts given the win. The French stuck by Pélissier and threatened to leave the race as well. Pélissier had even packed his bags when his wife Madeleine heard what had happened and placed what was then a difficult long-distance phone call to insist that he change his mind. He was the hero of his country, she insisted, and she was right. No rider had ever been so popular. He was also pigheaded, she said, and she was right there as well.

Madame Pélissier was a dominant woman, and her husband crumbled before her, and the French team before Pélissier. The riders stayed in the race. Next day their chance came when Binda crashed. The French attacked and got six riders into the winning break. Since there were only eight in the group, the other two, Guerra and the Belgian Jef Demuysere, could do nothing to slow it down. The break got so much of a lead that Binda finished 73rd and fell to 50th place overall, with more than an hour's disadvantage.

Now Binda had something else to complain about and again he insisted he was going home. But in the absence of a wife to nag him into staying in the race, it was Italian journalists who changed his mind. Emilio Colombo, the boss of the sports paper *Gazzetta dello Sport*, was following the race and told him bluntly that he didn't have the right to quit. Above all, he didn't have the right to go without doing something impressive first.

Binda shrugged. *"Va bene. Dopo, vediamo,"* he said "All right, I'll carry on." But it wasn't with enthusiasm. Next day he won the sprint at Pau ahead of Pélissier, then next day beat Leducq and Pierre Magne, the only two riders able to stay with him on the Pyrenean stage to Luchon. And then he got off his bike and went home, just as things were going well. Why he did it stayed a mystery for decades. People don't just throw in the Tour de France when they're on a roll. Binda broke the silence of half a century when he confessed to journalists in his apartment in the via Juvara in Milan on the eve of the Giro in 1980:

"I didn't want to use up my energy in the Tour," he said. "In the end I was forced into it. Emilio Colombo came to see me as an emissary of Henri Desgrange. Desgrange wanted me in the Tour to give it extra prestige in its new formula [of national rather than trade teams]. I wasn't very keen and Desgrange offered me a contract equivalent to what I'd get for riding a track meeting. My rate for each stage was what I'd have been paid in a vélodrome. He knew I wouldn't get as far as Paris."

Colombo, presumably in on the deal, would have known that Desgrange would want rather more for his money than a few days' tantrums. When he said Binda didn't have the right to walk out, "without doing something impressive first," it may well have been financial acumen rather than Italian pride that he was referring to.

The most famous tug-of-war in bike racing is the one that won Benoni Beheyt the World Championship in his native Belgium in 1963. It was perhaps intended to be one of the most profitable maneuvers ever, but it backfired on Benoni. Sadly for him, the man he denied was the Belgian "emperor", Rik van Looy, a man with round eyes, a Halloween smile, short shorts on his massive thighs, a way of sprinting like a cat pouncing on a mouse, and a terrible habit of not taking snubs lightly. Van Looy's influence in Belgium was so great that Beheyt's career effectively ended the day that it peaked.

The story is that in 1963, Beheyt, from the Flemish town of Zwijnaarde, had just ridden his first Tour de France. He was in the black and green of the Wiel's Groene-Leeuw team, backed by a brewery and a bike firm, and finished 49th, having expected no better. The Tour ended on Bastille Day, July 14. Jacques Anquetil was feted across France for winning by 3:35 over Federico Bahamontes, the Spanish climber, but Beheyt went home unnoticed, another foot-soldier, known only for winning Ghent–Wevelgem.

The World Championship came four weeks after the Tour, on August 11. It was held at the Belgian town of Ronse, and nobody doubted a Belgian — any Belgian, but probably van Looy — would win in front of a home crowd. But there were problems. Belgium is only a small country, just a couple of hours' drive from one side to the other, but most bike-racing is crammed into the northern, Dutch-speaking, half called Flanders. The important teams and most of the best riders were all based in Flanders, and rivalry in the hothouse of Belgian cycling was intense.

The Belgian selectors did what they always did and picked their team to provide a good result, but above all to placate the sponsors. As usual, the routine was to pick the best riders from each team, then at least one other rider to support the main man. Then the whole lot would be asked to overcome their day-to-day rivalry and work for the glory of the kingdom. If the glory of the kingdom didn't work, then threats and bribery often would.

Van Looy didn't need to threaten. Everyone knew he was the clear favorite, a man whose speed won him around 500 victories and almost every single-day classic, including Paris–Roubaix three times. He had won four stages of that year's Tour, including the last one into Paris. Everyone also knew that his influence went far beyond each race, that his popularity in criteriums, the main money-spinner for workaday riders, was enough that promoters were tempted to deny contracts to riders against whom Van Looy didn't care to compete. You upset him at your peril, in other words.

If he didn't need to threaten, he *was* prepared to bribe. To anyone prepared to help him win a third World Championship, he said, he would pay $500 if he won the rainbow jersey. That was a striking sum in 1963. Economic History Services says it would be worth $2,900 in 2002, to which you have to add the fact that in 1963 many riders in professional teams weren't paid at all. An offer of $2,900 to lose a bike race to someone who would probably have beaten you anyway is pretty persuasive.

But things can change in the heat of the moment. To be fair, I don't know whether Beheyt had agreed to take van Looy's money. Nor can anyone remember now whether the deal was that individuals would sign in advance for van Looy's personal squad or if those who helped would be singled out afterwards and given their bonus. The second seems more likely.

What happened was that the bunch came down toward the finishing straight with the force of a water mill in full flood. Out of it briefly came another Belgian, Gilbert Desmet, who had attacked more to show himself trying to win in a hopeless situation than with any hope of success.

If van Looy had thought the race was going the way he wanted, he suddenly found out that it wasn't. For one thing he found the British rider Tom Simpson in the way and gave him a great tug to get by. Then, as Simpson recounted: "Van Looy was shouting desperately for someone to give him a wheel to pace him to the front. He asked Benoni Beheyt but was told he had cramp. Beheyt was foxing and, taking the inside, had gone to the front under his own power.

"As I was told, van Looy saw him and switched across the road trying to ward him off. Just about side by side, Beheyt got hold of van Looy's jersey and I reckon he must have said to himself 'Should I *push* him? Should I hell!' And so he *pulled* him as his captain was trying to push him away, and he took the title by inches. A perfect example of the biter being bitten."

Van Looy was diplomatic, and shrugged off the incident with surprising coolness. But he or Beheyt — probably both — already realized that Beheyt's career was over. He would be consigned to the exclusive trash bin of undeserving World Champions, like the Dutchman Harm Ottenbros, of whom more in a moment.

Beheyt and van Looy were in different teams, Beheyt with Wiel's and van Looy first with GBC-Libertas and then the stronger Solo-Superia, and van Looy was in no position to keep Beheyt out of the Tour de France. That was for individual team managers to decide, and Beheyt even won the stage from Orléans to Versailles in 1964 and the same year's Tour of Belgium. But he never again won where van Looy had any say. He gave up: he stopped racing in 1967, just 26 years old. He had just 19 wins as a professional, the biggest and the most destructive his world title.

Benoni Beheyt still helps at races and runs the radio link on Liège–Bastogne–Liège. Winning the World Championship as an unknown may have ruined his career, but it didn't ruin his life, as it did to poor Harm Ottenbros.

Ottenbros also won his World Championship title in Belgium, at Zolder, on 10 August 1969, as an unknown 26-year-old. Where Belgium wanted van Looy in 1963, it was even more sure that Eddy Merckx would win in 1969. But there was such determination among other riders that Merckx should *not* win and dominate cycling still further, that his every move was negated and he got off in despair to the whistles and jeering of fans.

Ottenbros would normally have ridden for the Dutch favorite, Jan Janssen, but Janssen had pulled out sick. That freed Ottenbros and, in a race denied its big names, he got away in the last four kilometers with Belgian rider Julien Stevens. Ottenbros won by centimeters, and managed what Jacques Anquetil, Gino Bartali, Sean Kelly, and many others more worthy never achieved: a World road title.

I was working at *Cycling* in central London that afternoon. Alan Gayfer, the editor, looked at the first reports of the race from his reporter at Zolder and threw the whole lot in the air in despair.

"World Champion?" he scoffed. "He wouldn't harm a fly."

The rainbow jersey proved all but worthless to Ottenbros. He earned no more as World Champion — $2,500 — than he had as a criterium rider. The only rider to congratulate him was Franco Bitossi, during the Tour of Lombardy. Ottenbros was so touched that he gave him one of his jerseys.

Riders ganged up to stop him winning even criteriums. They sneered at his lack of talent on the hills and called him the "Eagle of Hogerheide," an ironic reference both to Federico Bahamontes, the "Eagle of Toledo," and the unrelenting flatness of the Dutch countryside where he lived.

"That nickname made me more famous than my World Championship," he says now.

Ottenbros broke his wrist in the next year's Tour of Flanders, and could neither ride the spring classics nor defend his title. Then his team, sponsored by the cigar maker Willem II, announced that it was folding, and Ottenbros retired, depressed and considering suicide.

In 1976 he rode across the Zeeland bridge in southwest Holland with a Dutch rider of the new generation, Gerrie Knetemann. Together they halted, and Ottenbros picked up his bike, lifted it over the parapet and threw it into the river. He watched it fall through the water in circles before disappearing. Then he finished the journey home perched on Knetemann's top tube.

Life took a bitter turn. His marriage broke up and he lost touch with his children. He drove around France, trying to find himself and what he had once been, then lived in a squat in Sliedrecht, near Rotterdam, sleeping on a mattress on the floor.

"I had money in the bank," he says, "but I never touched it. I wanted nothing to do with cycling and that life, the self-centered life, that led to my divorce."

He took up sculpture but abandoned it when people wanted to buy what he created. He was scared of becoming well-known again. He now lives in an unremarkable housing area of Dordrecht, doing a succession of odd jobs to make ends meet. Some days he glues tiles to walls and floors, other days he fits carpets. In his spare time he works with mentally handicapped children.

He rides a bike again, for the fun of it, and makes appearances with other bygone Dutch stars, such as Jan Janssen and Jo de Roo. "But," he says, "if I could live my life all over again, I'd miss out the cycling bit."

To return to Beheyt, you will remember that he rode for Wiel's-Groene Leeuw. If what happened to Beheyt was dubious, what happened to a great part of the team in 1962 was even odder. The Tour stage from Luchon to Carcassone set off 10 minutes late because Wiel's sunken-cheeked German rider Hans Junkermann had been ill most of the night. At first he wasn't going to start in the morning. Then he decided he would, and the Tour, not wanting to lose a man who was both eighth overall and a team leader, gave him the extra 10 minutes. The 116 riders then bowled away.

They didn't ride that fast. They rarely do at the start of the day, and anyway they had been asked not to. The bunch sympathized with Junkermann, especially a surprising number of others who also weren't feeling too bright that day. Carcassone is a medieval hilltop town between Toulouse and the Mediterranean, the weather was hot, and there was no point in rocketing away. However slowly they went, though, Junkermann slid to the back of the field. At 50 km he lost contact on the first climb and collapsed. And there he sat by the road, his face more gaunt than ever, his bike beside him, onlookers gathered around him looking distressed.

"Bad fish at the hotel," he mumbled. "I was sick from it all night." Eleven others left the race that day, also blaming bad fish. They included Willy Schroeders who had been the Yellow Jersey at Bordeaux a few days earlier, and the 1960 winner, Gastone Nencini, a conspicuous drug-taker. It wasn't much of an excuse. It was obvious that the first thing any decent journalist would do is check with the riders' hotels. They did, and the hoteliers didn't much like being accused of poisoning a sizable proportion of the Tour de France. None of them had served fish, they protested with some glee, drawing the same conclusions as Pierre Dumas, the Tour doctor, and enjoying the mischief of revenge. Dumas quickly decided the riders had consumed more than just wholesome food. "Certain preparations" was how he put it. It was less *poisson* (fish) than poison.

The papers had fun with the story for days and enjoyed the way in which supposedly intelligent men had concocted an excuse guaranteed to fall apart upon first examination. Team managers reacted angrily, accusing Dumas of a slur, but knowing they were on less than dependable ground. As the French manager Marcel Bidot had said, so many riders were still high on drugs when he visited their rooms in the evening that they scared him. Riders threatened to strike for 15 minutes, although it was hard to know on what grounds, which was probably the point the scholarly Jean Bobet made when he dissuaded them from doing so.

The most open campaigner for the freedom to take drugs was five-time Tour winner Jacques Anquetil. The French journalist Pierre Chany always praised him, if not for taking drugs, then at least for having the pride and honesty to say what he had taken. He "never dropped his eyes and looked ashamed and shifty like other riders," he said.

Anquetil not only won five Tours, but also nine Grands Prix des Nations, the 140 km time-trial on the outskirts of Paris that held the status of a World Championship, including six in a row from 1953 to 1958. It's a record never likely to be bettered, even now that the race is only 100 km and run on different courses around France. At least one of those unofficial World Championships was helped by an 80 km/h push from a car.

Anquetil was a complex man, much shaped by his childhood and his father. He grew up in a rustic roadside cottage in the countryside outside Rouen. It was a single-story building with little doors and windows and an open fire and exposed beams inside. "The sort of house that tourists find pretty, but those who live in them find uncomfortable," he recalled.

His father was a stubborn and occasionally spiteful man, the sort who would make his own life less comfortable rather than oblige someone he disliked. That, not unreasonably, was how it was when the Germans invaded northern France at the start of World War II. The Germans wanted him to

Jacques Anquetil was known not only for his hard work, willpower, and determination, but also as an apologist for drug-taking.

carry on working as a stonemason. Because the Germans wanted him to, Ernest Anquetil didn't want to. He refused. It put him out of work, but he had stuck to his principles. He went to work instead with his brothers, who were strawberry-farmers. Anquetil junior helped on the smallholding. He didn't have much choice: his father set him to work at the age of six.

That was the background when the son got interested in cycling and joined the club at Sotteville, a region of Rouen on the banks of the Seine. There he came under the influence of another bossy, controlling man: André Boucher, who turned the round-faced and gangly youngster into a champion. But his technique was dictatorial and Anquetil rebelled.

"Boucher had turned the ACSS [the local cycling club] into a severe club where bans flourished," he remembered. "That was a good method for many of the other members, but not for me. I only have to look at a wall that's holding me in, making me a prisoner, to want to jump over it. It's almost a reflex action. If cigarettes were banned, I would smoke. We couldn't go out in the evenings? I went out. If flirting was against the rules, I flirted."

On the other hand, Anquetil rarely missed the club's gym sessions, leading Boucher to reproach those who did, pointing out that Anquetil had ridden 10 km from Quincampoix, whereas they had to come from only just around the corner. That combination of determination, willingness to suffer, enthusiasm for principles, but reluctance to accept rules he didn't share embroiled him in so many doping rows that to this day, the French feel uneasy about remembering him as a hero.

## Deals, Anyone?

Do riders still do deals before World Championships?
Yes they do, according to Paolo Bettini of Italy in 2001: "On the eve of the World Championships we hold a meeting to establish the win bonus that we'll divide among the other members of the team if one of us wins. The figure is around $120,000, maybe more if someone is extra-confident, and it also depends on what the Italian Cycling Federation has put up. It's a financial consolation to reward the work of those who contributed to winning but won't benefit from any of the spin-offs."

The man who brought the 19-year-old Anquetil to the Grand Prix des Nations for the first time was Francis Pélissier. Of the three brothers, Charles has already turned up in our story, and the other, Henri, infuriated everyone so much that in the end his lover shot him using the gun that Henri's wife had turned on herself in her own misery.

Francis Pélissier had a reputation as a picker of winners and the nickname of "Sorcerer" for always working magic on those in his charge. Have him in your camp, and you knew you'd arrived. Have him in your camp, and you also got as much help as the rules allowed — and perhaps more than they allowed.

Anquetil won the first Nations as an outsider, not even a full professional, and he thought he could count on Pélissier for ride number two. Instead, Pélissier put his bets on another of his riders, the elegant Swiss Hugo Koblet, who held the course record. Anquetil was consigned to the team mechanic, a fact that hurt him all the more for having to find out himself through workshop gossip.

There was more than loss of pride and confidence. Anquetil was determined not to miss out on Pélissier's trick in the feeding area and he promised the mechanic a roasting if he didn't oblige in the same way. "In the feeding area, Francis was unbeatable," Anquetil admitted. "The area was 500 meters long. The rider would hang on to the car and Pélissier would drop something into his pockets. But above all, he would drive through the feeding area at 80 km/h…"

The rule has long since changed, perhaps because Pélissier was rumbled, but it shows how an experienced and less than scrupulous manager can help where he feels it's needed. And Anquetil's mechanic promised he had learned the trick.

Despite two punctures in four kilometers, Anquetil won the race, riding the last quarter "as if I was inhuman, a machine, a mad robot." What's more he not only beat Koblet but bettered his record by 52 seconds. Which prompted his moment of revenge: "That same evening," Anquetil said, "I sent my winner's wreath to Mrs. Francis Pélissier, offering my condolences."

# 7. Mostly Mischief

Perhaps there's such a thing as innocent cheating. Funny cheating, anyway. Take Britain's Tom Simpson, for example.

Simpson was contracted to ride the Madrid Six Day in Spain with the Australian rider John Tressider. The old idea of having a rider from each team on the track for all 24 hours a day had died out everywhere else but Madrid. The race was neutralized from 4 AM to 10 AM to avoid exhausting chases in front of empty seating of the sort that had infuriated Louis Delblat at the Vel' d'Hiv', but still riders had to lap the track gently. Sometimes they rode with just one leg, the other foot steering the handlebars as they used their leg to support the letters they were writing. Sometimes they shaved as they went or read newspapers. But always they were both bored and tired.

Simpson was a comedian and a man quick to spot a crafty way around problems. In Madrid, he was quick to spot that his thin face and rudder-like nose were remarkably like those of his mechanic and assistant, David Nice, an enthusiast from Colchester in eastern England whom Simpson had met while racing in Belgium. The two had got on well, and Nice had traveled to Madrid with Simpson and Tressider to see Six Day racing from the inside and to earn himself some cash.

Simpson came up with an idea for services beyond the original engagement, offered him a bonus, dressed him in his own tracksuit, put a scarf round the bottom of his face (which riders did as the stadium grew cold) and topped him off with a favorite Russian, which hat he had bought years earlier in Moscow.

"He was me to anyone giving a cursory glance at the figures plodding round the track," Simpson recalled.

Nice rode nervously on to the track but either nobody spotted the ruse or they were prepared to stay quiet about it. Round and round he went while Simpson and Tressider got a good night's sleep. It seems unlikely that the other riders didn't know what was going on. They may have objected to rivals being in bed while they had to trundle pointlessly around the foot of the boards, but they would also have enjoyed the mischief and the way it cocked a snook at the organizers.

The track manager, unfortunately, was also a cyclist, and was prepared to stay up at night so that he could meet the stars he admired but rarely got a chance to talk to. Spotting what he thought was the talkative Simpson, he rode his own bike up to him and started to talk to him in the one language they shared.

Simpson recalled: "He chatted away quite happily to Dave, whose French was near enough nonexistent. Well, it was not long before he sensed something was wrong and whipped the scarf off the poor lad's face. He stormed over to my cabin and dragged me out, half asleep, on to the track. That was that! He and the other officials kept their eyes on us after that and we had little chance of getting away with any more larks like that."

There was mischief in the mind of the Dutchman Rini Wagtmans, too, during the 1969 Tour. Wagtmans, whose streak of white hair in the center of his forehead gave him the nickname *Kuifje*, or Tufty, spent most of his career as a domestique for Eddy Merckx. He gave up many of his own chances for his leader, therefore, but he was good enough to come fifth in the 1970 Tour and third in the 1969 Vuelta. He also wore the Yellow Jersey in 1970.

In 1969 he was on his way to finishing sixth, not yet riding for Merckx but in the Willem II team for which Harm Ottenbros had ridden. He was not a classic climber, but he was a spectacular descender, an ability he had shown in the Alps and Pyrenees.

That day the stage left Clermont-Ferrand, the Michelin tire-making town in eastern France, for Montargis. After that there was just one more day, a conventional race from Montargis to Creteil in the morning and the closing time-trial into Paris in the afternoon. Wagtmans wasn't likely to win any of those or overall, but he had nothing left to lose from a stunt in the race's dying hours.

Even so, nobody expected him — or anybody else — to attack so early. It was so soon that the race hadn't even formally started. The race was still ambling through the neutralized section before the *départ réel* in the city outskirts. Riders were still inquiring after each other's health and discussing what they'd read in the papers and generally getting comfortable when they were startled to see a flash of royal blue. Wagtmans had broken away.

He raced past the red car of an angry and gesticulating Jacques Goddet at the head of the race, pushed on towards the motorcycle outriders from the *gendarmerie* clearing a way through Clermont, and slammed his bike into the highest gear he could turn. And then, weaving through the city like a demon, he spotted what he wanted: a side-turning. He tugged on the brakes, his back wheel all but skidding, slipped his feet out of the toe clips and ran into the alleyway. And there he hid.

Back in the bunch, nobody knew what to do. Certainly it was against the rules to attack in the neutralized area but that wasn't the moment to gamble that the judges would do what they were supposed to do. Then the Frenchman Lucien Aimar, never a man to take offense lightly, set off in angry chase. Aimar, too, couldn't be ignored because he'd won the Tour three years earlier, in 1969.

When Aimar went, everyone else went as well. At the front they knew what was going on. At the back, still digesting their breakfast and waving to the crowd, they had no idea. Those at the front were just angry; those at the back were at the very least offended as they found themselves clinging to a long snaking line of riders thrashing through the part of town they were supposed to negotiate gently. All they could do was grit their teeth and wonder what was going on.

Wagtmans knew the upset he would cause. What he hadn't predicted, though, was that it would unfold so spectacularly. His idea was to wait until the whole field had trundled past at club-run speed and then make his way back up through the following cars before having a laugh with his pals. Instead, the race went so fast in its angry and imaginary pursuit that he couldn't get back on fast enough. Far from chuckling at his ruse, he was reduced to chasing the race for miles, his face grimacing and his teeth clenched.

But then, practical jokes ran in the family. The Wagtmans family is well known in St.-Willebrord, the village on the Belgian border north of Antwerp which was home to some of Holland's greatest cycling stars. Rini's uncle was Wout Wagtmans, who died in 1994. He was the first Dutchman to win an important foreign stage race, leading the Tour of Romandy from beginning to end in 1952, and he seemed to be poised to win the Tour de France in 1956 — until he cracked in the Alps.

"I wore the Yellow Jersey for 13 days," he recalled, "and I was one of the favorites to win. Then in the last but one stage, from Turin to Grenoble, it all went wrong, and I finished the day 30th and lost the jersey. Roger Walkowiak won the Tour. I still don't understand what happened that day. I was so close to winning, and that should give you wings. But not me."

Wagtmans lost the Tour to a Frenchman, which you would think would have pleased at least the French. But instead of a hero, they got the little-known Walkowiak, a last-minute selection in a regional team who was such an unpopular winner that Jacques Goddet said of the finish at the Parc des Princes that "The applause from spectators sounded like a lamentation." Walkowiak, who had just ridden the fastest Tour to date without winning a single stage, was so badly rattled that by 1958 he had moved from Tour winner to *lanterne rouge*.

However badly Wagtmans took his own disappointment, at least he knew how to have a good laugh, and he did — for the rest of his life. Not so Walkowiak. He raced for another two years, even winning a stage of the Tour of Spain in 1957, then realized, like Harm Ottenbros and Benoni Beheyt, that

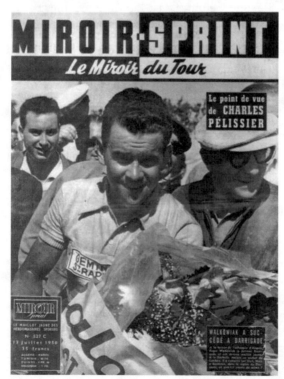

Roger Walkowiak's name has become synonymous with "undeserved winner" in French cycling circles. He took over the lead from Wagtmans in the 1956 Tour on the last mountain stage and rolled into Paris wearing the Yellow Jersey.

the greatest moment of his life had in fact been its worst. He suffered depression for years.

He opened a café in Montluçon but found that even his customers thought he'd been an unworthy winner. He slid deeper into gloom and suspicion and went back to the lathe of the car factory he had left only a decade earlier to become a Tour rider. To win the Tour *à la Walkowiak* still means to win against expectations and from the shadows.

Before we get back to the jolly japes, it may be worth mentioning that winning the Tour has also been the undoing of other riders. Hugo Koblet was a superb stylist, famous for grooming himself as he rode. He was getting a hard time from the Frenchman François Mahé in the 1951 Tour of Switzerland, and solved it by riding hands off in the mountains to run a comb through his hair. Mahé quickly dropped back, completely demoralized.

Koblet won the 1951 Tour de France with the help of a 135 km lone break from Brive to Agen, of which old-timers still talk with reverence. For all that Gino Bartali, Fausto Coppi, Louison Bobet and others chased, Koblet just cruised onwards. He won by 2:15, remembering to sit up in the finish straight to take out his sponge, bottle of cologne and comb to smarten himself up for his reception.

By 1953, though, he was a wreck. Jean Bobet, brother of Louison and the man who once dissuaded the alleged fish-poisoning victims from going on strike, said: "We saw him in 1953 getting an odd sickness above 2,000 m, then above 1,500 m, then above 1,000 m. We saw him unable to get over even the tiniest hill, and we were witnesses to his disappearance. His face grew older and his personality somber." The peloton in the Giro, remembering how great Koblet had once been, even waited for him after a crash.

On 2 November 1964, Koblet was driving his white Alfa-Romeo when it left a bend outside Zürich and hit a tree. Its speedometer was jammed at 120 km/h. He died three nights later, aged 39, having lost most of his money on elegant living and failed business ventures.

Equally troubled was the Spanish rider Luis Ocaña. He gave Eddy Merckx the hardest Tour ride of his life, as he teased and belittled him with his lone break through the Alps to Orcières-Merlette in 1971. He won the yellow jersey by nine minutes, as the bunch enjoyed the spectacle of the all-dominating Belgian being belittled and refused to help him chase.

Ocaña didn't win the Tour, because he crashed in a storm on the descent of the col de Mente as he and Merckx dueled in a bitter personal battle. Other riders crashed into Ocaña's back in the gloom, hitting him in the kidneys as he staggered back towards his bike, and he ended the race in hospital.

Two years later, in 1973, he won the Tour and six stages, but it was the year Merckx didn't ride, and Ocaña found himself considered a *faux* winner, as Joop Zoetemelk was when Bernard Hinault pulled out in 1980, and poor Walkowiak had been in 1956. His big wins ended with that Tour, and he retired in 1977 to settle on a farm at Mont-de-Marsan, the town in southwest France to which his father had moved in 1945. His life spiraled unrelentingly downwards, and on 19 May 1994, he lifted a rifle to his head and shot himself.

But I'm digressing from the theme of jolly japes. So here's another one:

Holland's first *maillot jaune*, Wim van Est, comes from the same village as the Wagtmans family and has one of the best story about Wout Wagtmans I have ever heard: "We were riding the Dutch club championship and we'd got an eight-minute lead," he said. "Five hundred meters before the line he saw a little children's bike and he got on it and pedaled across the line on that. The judges didn't get the joke and they disqualified us. But how we laughed."

For many years, the longest race in the world was Bordeaux–Paris. It's the race which Arthur Linton rode in his trembling and glassy-eyed state in 1896. What made it different from other races wasn't just the distance, around 600 km depending on each year's route, but the fact that it stayed faithful to the idea of having pacers when other events had long abandoned them.

It had a lot of prestige attached until the end of the 1960s. Wim van Est won it at its peak, in 1950, 1952, and 1961. It was a terrifying event because of

## Whatever Happened to... Bordeaux–Paris?

The Derby of the Road, as Bordeaux–Paris has often been called, ran from 1891 to 1896 behind human pacers, from 1897 to 1899 behind cars or motorbikes and occasional human pacers, returned to bicycle pacers from 1900 to 1930 (with a break for the war). It then turned to motorbikes from 1931 to 1937 before adopting the Derny in 1938. That remained the standard until 1986, 1987 and 1988, when there were no pacers at all. The race hasn't been organized since.

its importance, its distance, and the speed that riders maintained behind their Derny motorbikes. It took, er, special preparation... Van Est remembers:

> One of my Belgian team-mates spotted a little box on the front seat of our team manager's car. He could just make out that it held some sort of pills and he asked me if they'd be any good to get him through the race. He said he needed something strong to get him through something as hard as Bordeaux–Paris. So I picked up the box, gave him two of what was inside, and told him to take them a quarter of an hour before the start. And that's what he did. But two kilometers after the start he had to get off his bike.
>
> They weren't drugs in the box; they were flints for the manager's cigarette lighter.

The British rider Vin Denson also had to get off his bike. And also because of a little cheating.

The agreement in Bordeaux–Paris was always that riders would stay together through the night and then stop after dawn to strip to their race clothes before picking up their Dernys, usually in Châtellerault. That applied in 1965, the year that Jacques Anquetil was attempting the world's longest race only hours after winning the Dauphiné Libéré stage race. He drove straight from the finish of that, flew to Bordeaux in a hired Mystère 20 with just a nap on the way, then turned up at Quatre Pavilions in the suburbs where Bordeaux–Paris started. It was the stunt of a lifetime.

Anquetil had hired Denson, his teammate in the Ford team, to protect his interests. In particular he was to watch out for Tom Simpson, who was

## Whatever Happened to... Vin Denson?

Denson's career went to pieces with the death of his friend Tom Simpson in the 1967 Tour de France. The loss hit him so hard that he was in no condition to take up the offer to win the next day's stage alone as a tribute to his lost teammate.

He raced another year on the Continent, rode again for a couple of chaotic years with the semi-professionals in Britain, then retired to start a timber-treatment business near Harlow, north of London. He still rides a bike, still brims with stories, and races as an amateur.

Denson's best friend and a pal of Anquetil's, but nevertheless a rival from the Peugeot camp.

There was more than the usual interest when the race left Bordeaux, because of Anquetil's impending double. The Frenchman had had a hard time in Dauphiné Libéré because other riders, notably Raymond Poulidor, had attacked him repeatedly, knowing he would be tempted not to respond because of the Bordeaux–Paris to follow. There was even speculation that he might pull off the whole trick, which his manager, Raphaël Géminiani, had clinched by appealing to his pride: "You're the Emil Zátopek of cycling," he said, referring to the Czech runner who had won the 5,000 m, then the 10,000 m, and then the marathon at the 1952 Olympic Games in Helsinki. It was an event Anquetil remembered well because he had been there, riding the team time-trial for France.

The initial interest over, though, the race settled into the monotony of 150 miles in the glare and shadows of following headlights which exaggerated the sweeping rain and made everyone miserable. Nobody broke away, as agreed, but unknown to the others, the Frenchman Claude Valdois had changed his clothes in the darkness at the back of the group. He attacked when the others stopped to get out of their own wet clothes in the limited privacy of opened car doors.

Derny races on the road are still held these days. This shows the modern versions in action during a race in the Netherlands around 1980.

"Everybody saw him go and a cry of 'the bastard' went up and it was pandemonium," said Simpson. He was furious because Valdois was his teammate and had been briefed to attack by Peugeot's manager, Gaston Plaud, who had not told Simpson, the team's leader. Anquetil was furious because the whole field had been duped. He doubtlessly thought that Simpson was in on the deal, and saw it as duplicity by his closest rival.

"Valdois literally caught us with our pants down," Denson recalled. "I jumped after him with my shorts half on, fastening my braces [suspenders],

## Whatever Happened to... Dernys?

The Derny was a half-bike, half-motorbike, originally made by Roger Derny and his sons in small workshops around Paris. They were struck by the clumsiness of the monster belt-driven motorbikes they had seen at the Vélodrome d'Hiver and the Parc des Princes and thought there ought to be a better way, especially on the road.

The family had been cyclists and ran a shop that sold both bikes and motorbikes. They merged the ideas in 1936 and created a thing with a sloping top tube, a down tube that bent in a lazy L towards the bottom bracket, the whole thing stressed by a stiffening bar that ran diagonally from the head tube to the rear axle.

It had a 98 cc two-stroke engine and a fixed gear which had to be turned all the time the clutch was engaged, the saddle was from a racing bike and set very low to protect the rider behind, there was no silencing, the exhaust belched oil fumes, and the handling was tricky because the 28-inch rear wheel had a narrower tire than the smaller wheel in front. The trademark was the barrel of fuel carried, in the manner of a St-Bernard dog, in front of the handlebars.

The first roadworthy version emerged in 1937 and production continued until 1956, at which time the Derny factory was in the avenue du Général Michel Bizot in the 12th *arrondissement*.

The surviving machines lingered on another two decades, by which time they were undependable and slow. Modern versions are now made in Neepelt, Belgium, by the engineer Arie Simon, but Roger Derny and his sons would quickly recognize their original design.

and Stablinski, the other Ford man riding for Anquetil, followed with one sock on and still trying to get his heels in his shoes."

Simpson, meanwhile, had lost one of the men he was counting on to support him against Anquetil. Valdois the supporter had become Valdois the "stupid nit," as Simpson put it with understatement. He recalled: "I took my shoes off to change my sodden socks, having a clean vest and a jersey on, when suddenly I saw a Peugeot rider go away. I struggled to get into my shoes again, still wearing the dirty socks, and I had considerable difficulty. The back of one shoe folded down and I had no shoehorn so stood there at the roadside minus my shorts, trying to get my shoe on. At last I succeeded and hurriedly pulled on my clean pants, already greased."

In those days shorts were made of closely woven wool and had genuine chamois leather inserts. The leather had to be treated before each race with a coating of lanolin, without which it became stiff and unusable but with which, unfortunately, it became a breeding ground for germs and encouraged saddle sores.

"As I was belting off up the road, I thought, 'What on earth is this?' What had happened was that, as I had put on my shorts, gravel from my socks and shoes had stuck in the grease and was now hurting like the devil. So there I am, riding along digging my hands inside my shorts and pulling out lumps of gravel. I was still scraping gravel off my behind for some miles."

Denson wasn't much better off, also adjusting his clothes as he went, but he had another problem. He had calculated on having a pee, a luxury he had missed since Bordeaux several hours back. He and his bulging bladder caught Valdois just before Châtellerault and won the customary prize for being first to reach the Dernys. His pacer, a man called Pleasance, was waiting in the road with his engine running and the pair set off for Paris with another Derny rider behind them in case Pleasance broke down or needed a break.

Valdois was also there with his own pacers and the noisy party buzzed along at more than 40 mph. "I think he had rosy dreams of us winning the race," Denson said. But the Englishman was there to protect his leader's interest, in this year above all, not to grab glory himself. Nevertheless they built a respectable lead.

"We were five minutes up," Denson remembers, "when, in agony, I could no longer ignore the insistence of nature and I called to Pleasance to stop. 'You can't stop in Bordeaux–Paris,' he cried, to which I replied 'Watch me!' and I lined up at a tree."

With nothing yet happening where the stars were, the press and newsreel photographers were up with Denson and Valdois. Grateful for something to film so early in what, for them, was a tedious race, they gathered around Denson, his tree and his lowered shorts. They were joined by journalists, race officials, the embarrassed and despairing Pleasance, several fascinated passersby, and a wintertime gravedigger called Bernard Stoops who worked each summer as a rider's *soigneur*. He was there to get Denson through the race.

The little crowd began urging Denson on like a racehorse, which did nothing for Denson's plumbing, pounded as it was by hours of riding through the rain all night. For five minutes he stood hopelessly by his tree as the cameras whirred and the cheers continued. The lesser lights began droning past behind their big-bellied pacers. Worse, along came Anquetil, the very man whom Denson had been employed to protect. Worse still, Anquetil and his pacer, the former rider Jo Gotourbe, were already locked in what turned out to be a 200-mile battle with Simpson.

More miserable than ever and still unsatisfied, Denson hauled up his shorts and set off once more, not only behind Pleasance but, worse, behind Anquetil. But it was still no use. Thirty miles later he got off again. The delighted reporters circled him once more, joined by Pleasance, Stoops, and a fresh set of onlookers.

"This time I had an unrewarding three minutes," Denson recalled with a mix of agony and amusement, "until the soigneur [Stoops] came up and did the trick with the aid of hot coffee on a sponge."

I have no idea what, if anything, Anquetil said to Denson when they next met. Maybe nothing. Stablinski had taken over the job that Denson was supposed to have done, and rode with his leader as Simpson tried to figure out what to do next.

"I was snookered because they were teammates, and so I was well and truly hammered. I took quite a hiding as first Stablinski and then Anquetil attacked. I had to go every time and gradually they wore me down. Some miles before the finish, Anquetil went away and I could not hold him."

Simpson finished third and had to be helped off his bike at the Parc des Princes. Denson probably just lay low for a while.

# 8. More Jolly Japes

There was a soldier, about a hundred years ago called Louis Trousselier. He was a good cyclist, and because of that his officers at the French 101st Regiment, where he was doing his compulsory service, let him go off when he requested leave to ride a bike race. What they did not know, and what young Louis didn't tell them, was that the race was the Tour de France, and that it would last rather longer than the 24 hours' leave they had allowed him.

The brass-hats soon realized what was going on when they read about it in the papers. Trousselier won five stages and by Bordeaux he was unbeatable. The race in 1905 was run on points rather than time and all Trousselier had to do was stay upright and get to the finish.

The organizer, Henri Desgrange, thought judging the race on points would offset the effect of one of his other rule, that riders must repair their own bikes in case of a breakdown. He forbade them from taking a spare bike or wheel without proving to judges that the damage had been beyond repair. There are many tales of riders cycling to the next control or even for hours to the finish with a broken bike on their shoulder or a smashed wheel strapped to their back. In fact in 1921 when Léon Scieur broke 11 spokes and rode 300 km with a wheel banging on his spine, he reckoned the dip in the bone was still there years later.

Anyway, repairs could take a lot of time and victories could be lost or won through simple misfortune, so Desgrange said it would be fairer to judge a rider by the order in which he finished rather than the time that it took him. The unforeseen consequence of the rule was that while a rider leading on time could always be beaten, if only theoretically, it's possible to reach a stage where a rider has so many points that he could finish last on every remaining stage and still win the race.

That was why Trousselier was unbeatable, and why he knew he had won the bonus promised by his sponsor, Peugeot, and why post-race contracts began coming in before the Tour was over. All this on top of the 6,950 francs he had in prizes. In all, he won 25,000 francs, which would be about $6,000 today, but the fortune of a lifetime in an era when an ordinary soldier would not have very high expectations.

And what did he do? He stopped off at the Buffalo track in Paris and sat around a massage table with two friends all night and gambled the lot away at cards and dice. "By the time Trousselier left the cabin," said Georges Berretrot, the announcer who had invented the idea of primes from the crowd, "he didn't have a sou in his pocket. He'd lost everything he'd suffered to win on the road. He'd had the joy of winning the Tour de France, and he'd been delighted to win. And to his credit, he accepted his losses without a grumble and had only one thought — to get back on his bike and win some money all over again."

To be fair, it did probably also cross his mind what would happen when he got back to his barracks, but then Trousselier — *"Trou-Trou"* ("hole- hole") as the French called him — wasn't a man much inclined to worry about trouble, or his money, or for that matter other people's money.

Trousselier was the master of the Free Meal Trick. It would probably work even today, and it certainly worked for Trousselier at Melun, Fontainebleau, Rombouillet, and a dozen other places. The routine was for Trousselier and two or three friends to go for a ride and then, come noon when the French traditionally have lunch, cruise through town looking for the most expensive restaurant. And there they would sit, possibly recognized by the *patron* as big racing stars, and they would order the most expensive meals on the menu.

As they ate, they would start arguing, and as the argument went on, so their voices would rise. Other diners would look across in concern, and before long the restaurant owner would ask if everything was all right. To which one of the riders would explain that they were discussing which of them was the fastest rider and that it had become terribly important for them to find out. Could the *patron* perhaps suggest a landmark a kilometer or two down the road to which the friends could race, turn round and then sprint back to the restaurant? That would settle the row. The restaurant owner could judge the result and the losers would pay for the meal. Time and again the *patron* would agree, and time and again the friends would disappear down the road, never to be seen again.

Trousselier not only won the Tour in 1905, but Paris–Roubaix the same year, and Bordeaux–Paris in 1908. He retired to work in his family's flower shop on the boulevard Haussman, the Parisian avenue named after Georges Haussman, the architect who between 1852 and 1870 swept away many of Paris's narrow alleys and replaced them with parks, wide boulevards and circular plazas.

Trousselier wasn't alone in scrounging a free meal or drink. Wim van Est remembered: "We didn't have any money in those days, and if you haven't got money, then you have to be crafty. When we went training, we had a trick to get ourselves a drink. We'd get to a shop and one of us would lie in the road as though he'd just fallen off and he'd start groaning in pain. Someone would always come out of the shop to see how he was and my friend in the gutter would ask for a drink and he'd always get one. Then he'd get up and we'd start riding again and further up the road we'd share out the drink between us. It solved the problem."

It's amazing how short of money professional bike riders were even in Van Est's time, the 1950s. He remembers traveling to races abroad, and not by car or plane. "It'd take two, three days in a train, sleeping in the netting racks above the seats where people usually put their suitcases," he recalled. "And if you could, you'd buy a bit of steak from the local butcher and go into a café and ask if they'd cook it for you. If they wouldn't, you'd just eat it raw."

His fellow professional and club mate Adrie Roks recalled: "All you got was a bike and some jerseys and shorts. No salary. Money was what you had to earn on the bike. There was a masseur in the big stage races, but otherwise not. And there was never any medical care. And we didn't want a massage too often, either, because that cost money and you had to pay for it yourself."

Piet van Est, another of the family, remembered: "We got a pair of shorts and two jerseys. If those jerseys happened to be in the wash and you turned up in a different one, then there was hell to pay. And if you happened to crash and tear one, well that was something you had to pay for."

Piet van Est, by the way, isn't one of those grumblers about how hard things used to be. Under all the changes, he says, there is still one important thing that has stayed the same and always will: "The riders still have to ride terribly, terribly hard," he says. So hard, in fact, that it's hard to resist the temptation to help.

Bernard Sainz is the man behind the sobriquet "Dr. Mabuse." In the 1976 Tour de France, he was working as a soigneur with the GAN-Mercier team, led by the veteran Frenchman Raymond Poulidor and including the balding Dutchman Joop Zoetemelk. Poulidor is always remembered as the Eternal Second, because he rode the Tour 14 times and finished eight times in the first three but never as winner. In fact, the title and the sentiment ought to belong to Zoetemelk, who finished second six times to Poulidor's three, but then he didn't have Poulidor's slow-speaking charm and, more important in France, he wasn't French.

Unnoticed in the ten-man GAN-Mercier team was the Frenchman Michel Perin, riding as number 26. He was a decent climber and an excellent team-rider, but he crashed going down the first mountain the Alps. Sainz went to his help, but it took a long time for Perin to recover and he got back on his bike only with a lot of pain. There were three more cols to come, and Perin looked set for a long, lonely, and painful ride — especially since the race exploded on the next climb as the stars made their move.

In the GAN car with Sainz was one of the race *commissaires*, who were in the habit of joining team managers and soigneurs to keep an eye on them. That limited Sainz's scope. But not his quick thinking.

"In my youth," he recalled, "I took part in a number of car rallies, and I have to say that I was as happy on four wheels as I had been on two [Sainz was a talented amateur track rider until he had a bad crash], perhaps even more daring. Going down the col, I dropped back from the other vehicles, feigning lack of attention, making a show of re-tuning my car radio, and I lit a cigarillo. Then, suddenly, I accelerated to catch the other cars. I let the ash from the cigarillo drop on to my pants during the straight stretches, and I'd look down to brush it away and straighten up only as we went into the next bend."

All the way down he skidded round bends, driving heel-and-toe on the accelerator and brake like a rally driver, squealing the tires until the *commissaire* had had enough.

"I'd been warned that you drove too fast but this is more than I can bear," he told Sainz. "I can't carry on like this. Stop, please."

Relieved of the commissaire's attention, Sainz could start looking after the cut, bruised, and suffering Perin. But before that, he stopped at a bar and asked for several notepads, the small sort that waiters used to write down orders. And then he rejoined Perin, driving two hairpins ahead of him. He kept that up for the remaining cols and smiled as his rider eventually regained the *grupetto*, the bunch of non-climbers who ride just fast enough to finish within the time limit.

That evening Perin came to see Sainz.

## Who was... Dr. Mabuse?

Dr. Mabuse is the nickname of Bernard Sainz, a tall, bespectacled and owlish man described by *L'Équipe* as sulfurous. He was born in Rennes on 1 September 1943 and was a talented amateur track rider until his career ended with a crash.

He got the nickname Dr. Mabuse during his time in horse racing, when he was twice convicted of abusing animals. One of his horses, Soft Machine, caused amazement when it won a major race days after being beaten soundly in a far easier event.

He has been allied with teams and individual riders since the 1970s and claims credit for miracles of cycling, including the resurrection of Raymond Poulidor's career in 1971, and for reviving the career of Francesco Moser to enable him to take two world hour records.

Sainz has had numerous brushes with the law and his offices and home have been raided. In 1999 he was convicted of practicing medicine without a license. A case involving syringes of testosterone fizzled out when he claimed he used them to increase his own sexual energy. He is a friend of the Belgian rider Frank Vandenbroucke, who in 2002 claimed a drugs cache found at his home was for his dog.

Sainz says he is a believer only in alternative therapies such as homeopathy.

The nickname comes from the 1920s science-fiction film "The Death Rays of Dr. Mabuse," in which a criminal mastermind becomes rich through hypnotic powers. In a second film, he is an insane prisoner who masterminds criminal plots from his cell by writing gibberish.

"It was unbelievable," he said. "I hardly had to pedal when I was riding those cols behind you. All the spectators were pushing me."

"You're joking," Sainz protested with a straight face.

"No, no, honestly, it's true."

Sainz kept his poker expression. "No, it can't be. They only push the last rider. You just recovered without being aware of it. It's a tribute to your will-power."

Perin will know the truth now, but he did not at the time: Sainz had used the notepads to good effect. Over and over he had written: "This rider has a fever-pitch temperature. Please give him a push." And he had handed them out to every group of fans he'd passed.

Zoetemelk finished that Tour in yet another second place, and Poulidor came third, both of them behind Lucien van Impe, a curly-haired Belgian who made no secret of the fact that he would rather have been at home with his pet birds. He only rode, it was said, because his wife nagged him into it. Perin finished 40th at 1:8:30. That was all that was expected of him. More, even. Subterfuge had worked.

That result was at least genuine, for the podium places anyway. You have to make up your own mind about Perin, whether the time limit would have eliminated him without Sainz's notepad. The races that follow the Tour are less straightforward. For years, the post-Tour criteriums were the way that the riders made money. Teams paid little except to their leaders. As Bas Malipaard said: "I never knew what Jacques Anquetil earned. We used to see him some mornings with a white wine and something to eat when he didn't have a chance to earn some more money. We domestiques never used to see much of it. You'd be happy if you could just scrape together a reasonable income from racing."

That was why so many struggled to finish the Tour, why the American sports writer Jack Olsen wrote of the nameless, faceless domestique who "may have lost his toenails from the constant forward pressure in his cycling shoes, his backside may be pocked by suppurating ulcers and his mind so addled by amphetamine that he is not sure of his name, but he is a hero, a major athletic figure, a finisher in the Tour de France."

Get to the finish and a whole half-year of criteriums awaited, contracts already drawn up by the three big agents of the period, the Frenchmen Daniel Dousset and Roger Piel and the Belgian Jean van Buggenhout. Of the three, the most powerful and the most resented was Dousset, a half-Brazilian Mafia-lookalike who died to few tears in October 1997, when he was 80. Those he left behind remembered the control he had over their lives, how he could offer or withhold contracts, raise or lower fees, and even instruct his contracted riders to combine against those who displeased him.

There are still criteriums around Europe, of course, but not as many as there once were. Some are genuine, more in some countries than in others. Sometimes prizes are listed in the program but never awarded, the money going in prearranged amounts according to the contract and the wishes of sponsors, who would always rather have a local man or a national hero win.

Sometimes things don't go the way the puppeteers want. The Australian sprinter and *maillot vert* Robbie McEwen said in October 2002: "At Dortmund this year (…), the organizers wanted Erik Zabel to win a close sprint with me second. But we were the only riders on appearance money, so everyone else was riding a fair race. A group went away and Zabel shouted 'Robbie!' I had to get him to the front for the win." The help was repaid when Zabel arranged a contract for McEwen 20 km away in Unna the following weekend.

The Dutch rider John Talen told *Nieuwsblad* in Utrecht: "I don't go to a criterium to win. That isn't the intention. You can try as a small rider, but you will lose. The big names catch you." It was the rules of cycling, he shrugged.

Ad Coenrads, organizer of the big but declining Acht van Chaam race, also in Holland, said guardedly: "Of course the riders made some deals in the past. But sometimes it has gone wrong as well. In 1981, Roy Schuiten won when it was supposed to be the local hero, Johan van der Velde. But it was 'over and out' in the peloton for Schuiten after that." Meaning that riders do not take easily to those who buck a lucrative system.

The French rider Erwann Menthéour remembered his own period on the circuit for the Gonzo drug-addled state he was in for much of the time.

"Laurent Jalabert was making his show," he recalled of one event. "He had just finished fourth in the Tour de France and he had the green jersey on his shoulders, with a win at Mende on July 14 [Bastille Day, the big French holiday] as a bonus. Naturally the public wanted to see him in action.

"He broke away by himself, by agreement with the others, because the script of a criterium is written in advance. The first two places are shared out according to placings in the Tour, the most popular riders in the race, and to the local champion, who's given the right to show himself off. Places three to five are sorted out during the race and an amateur is generally allowed to get in the next five to please the local supporters.

"That day, though, nothing went the way it was planned. Jaja [Jalabert] was supposed to drop back to us, and the bunch was riding as a group to get up to him, his lead went up by a second a lap. Some riders started getting worried,

## What About... Criterium Racing?

The most notorious criterium in France was the Circuit de l'Aulne at Châteaulin in Brittany, says Erwann Menthéour. It was known in the peloton as the Grand Prix de la Chaudière, a *chaudière* being a heater or boiler in French but a significant drug-taker in bike slang. Menthéour recalls being told: "To ride the Circuit de l'Aulne on water, that would be blasphemy!" He said the routine in bygone days was for riders to gather in a hotel room for the ritual of *Tonton-tintin-riri-même*, sharing what they'd brought for a pre-race party.

Tonton and Tintin were Tonedrine and Pervitine, Riri meant Ritaline and Mémé was methedrine.

"An impressive number of fans stand in front of the hotel where the riders are staying, and the atmosphere is electric. When you go to get your number in the middle of that crowd, it's like going down into an arena. The incredible tension even pushes some riders to give themselves a second injection before the start. The result is that everyone rides at 70 km/h along the Aulne and climbs the famous Stang-ar-Garront at 45 km/h on the big ring and the chain on the 12 or 13. When I tried it again in training, the difference was amazing."

Leading riders, he said, had objected to drug controls in French criteriums, and so there weren't any.

Johan van der Velde, the lanky, long-haired Dutchman with the Raleigh team, said in 1989 of criteriums and the way riders tackled them: "Every day, another race. It was detestable but you had to win money. You'd be taking amphetamines every two or three days. In the Tour it was always the same thing: an injection in the morning and pills in the evening."

He paid the price. He went to jail for stealing lawnmowers and money from stamp machines to pay for his habit.

and the complaints flew. He wasn't respecting the rules. In the end a rider feigned a puncture so he could wait for him and calm him down a bit. But when he got up alongside him, Jaja told him: "What are you talking about? I've been waiting for you for the last ten laps!'"

But at least he rode all the course. It's not unknown for riders to jump off and skip a lap when the course goes into the countryside and there are no spectators about. As Menthéour says: "In this job there are certain forbidden things that can be allowed under certain conditions. Crunching a lap [cycling slang for skipping one] is allowed. Provided you've just had a good Tour de France."

Menthéour tried it on a long descent through a forest in the Bol d'Or des Monédières at Chaumeuil. He hadn't had a good Tour de France. He didn't even have much of a record. He was just having a hard time as the Swiss star of the time, Tony Rominger, pushed up the pace. He stopped among the trees, took a *flèchette* [shortened hypodermic] of amphetamine from his pocket and injected himself in the shoulder before jumping back in next lap. The riders weren't upset that he had charged himself up. That was permitted. What wasn't allowed was to take time off when your reputation didn't justify it.

"In this world of hypocrisy," he said, "there was hell to pay."

# 9. Sharp End of the Needle

That Menthéour, as described in the preceding chapter, could even start off with a hypodermic in his pocket in that criterium, and that Van Est's teammate in Bordeaux–Paris was prepared to take anything, no matter what it was provided it was dope, says a lot about bicycle racing. However much cyclists try to defend their sport and point out that other sports can be as bad but don't have the courage to test as frequently or as thoroughly, the fact remains that competitors have dropped dead, turned crazy, or spoken openly of drug-taking much more in cycling than in any other sport.

There are reasons, of course. The early enthusiasm for excess in both distance and speed, the way that cycling quickly became a way to earn money rather than a hobby for gentlemen... all that. It all helps explain the origins. But it doesn't change the facts.

Drugging competitors to get them through a long race, whatever the sport, was considered legitimate when bicycle racing was in its infancy. Consider the case of Tom Hicks in the Olympic marathon at St. Louis in 1904, for instance. That was in an era when running 26 miles was considered dangerously close to human limits. He was leading and running well until he got to the point three-quarters of the way through, which experienced runners know is the danger point. It's there that their blood-sugar runs out and they switch to running on body fat, a change that takes time and makes less power, i.e. speed, available. Today, runners call it "hitting the wall," but in 1904, the reason for this sudden change was not yet widely known.

Hicks' helpers looked on in horror as their man started to slow and then wobble. They ran into the road and gave him an injection. He lurched on only to encounter more trouble a couple of miles later. More injections followed, and a mouthful of brandy. They got him to 22 miles, but by then he was in a dreadful state and begged to be allowed to stop. And was he? No. His helpers forced him on.

He got to the stadium entrance, collapsed, and was injected and doused again with brandy, and set on his way to stagger across the line to win a gold medal. Americans took the first three places, Hicks covering the course in 3: 28:53 to win by six minutes.

He didn't collect his gold medal immediately, though, because by then he "hung between life and death," as reports put it. He didn't recover for another few days, and he never ran a marathon again. *The Olympic Games*, the history of the Games, edited by IOC president Lord Killanin and John Redda and first published in 1971, says: "Many people realized that Hicks was doped with sulphate of strychnine and cognac, but no one at that time dreamed of protesting."

Choppy Warburton had been dead for nine years by then, but it's worth remembering that he had been in athletics before moving into cycling. His experience of how long races were won would have moved into cycling with him. It was probably through men like him, who entered cycling from professional "pedestrianism" — that drugs and long bike races soon seemed to have become inseparable.

At first nobody thought it odd. It was something that happened when you turned professional, a secret of the trade, and many professional and amateurs alike may well have accepted that they would take drugs to keep up with the rest. It was a rite of passage. Some did it reluctantly and others didn't give a damn or saw it as part of the job, but there doesn't seem much doubt that most of them did it.

As Alex Zülle told *Süddeutsche Zeitung* years later, after the Festina scandal that nearly brought the 1998 Tour to an end: "I've been in this business a long time. As a rider, you feel tied into this system. It's like when you're driving. The law says there's a speed limit of 100 km/h, but everyone is driving at 120 km/h or faster. Why should I be the one who obeys the speed limit? So I had two options: either fit in and go along with the others or go back to being a house painter."

It has been that way all along. If the choice is between painting walls or laboring in fields or chiseling coal and living your dream of bike racing, why hesitate if the only condition is that you take what everyone else is taking?

If there *is* a good thing about early drugs it's that they were self-limiting. Strychnine improves muscle tone, but there's a downside to taking too much. The same went for amphetamine, which the European Commission says first appeared at the Berlin Olympics in 1936. More specifically, the drug was Benzedrine, which had been isolated from amphetamine in the United States two years earlier. For the sake of simplicity, I'll use the word amphetamine to include Benzedrine and its allied drugs unless greater accuracy is needed.

Amphetamine seemed like the perfect drug. It made you feel great, it made you feel fresh where once you had felt tired, and it concentrated the mind. It made you obsessive, so you ignored the pain you felt, the risks you faced. It made your eyeballs the size of pinheads and you talked endless nonsense and your mouth made constant chewing motions, and you felt like a wreck when the stuff wore off, but as long as you were under its influence, it felt good and there seemed to be no serious aftereffects.

British troops used 72 million amphetamine tablets during World War II. Pilots and bomb crews used them so enthusiastically to overcome tiredness and sheer terror, that the pills had to be withdrawn. The crashed aircraft and wasted lives of the overly confident weren't worth the benefits.

Many who took them became addicted, or at any rate dependent. The effective dose rises quickly and, even if amphetamines are not addictive in the way of, say, heroin, they produce a feeling that nothing is possible without them. The best documented outbreak was in Japan, where the drug was unknown until servicemen began getting it during the war. The number of addicts, hardly any in 1945, rose to 200,000 in 10 years, plus presumably many more who hadn't registered. There were 5,700 admissions to mental hospital due to amphetamine psychosis in and around Tokyo in 1955. A third were still there a year later.

In the US alone, 8,000 million illegal amphetamine tablets were produced in 1966. That would be enough to give 5 mg almost every week to every man, woman, and child in the country. By then, riders in bike races had begun collapsing of it, a few had died of it, and one had been strapped down and taken to hospital in a raving state during the 1955 Tour de France.

Star riders could manage on just a small dose — not enough to keep them awake at night. Lack of sleep in the Tour is worse than any mountain climb. The more you feared not getting through the race at all, the more you were used as an expendable foot-soldier by the star who employed you, the more you were inclined to take. You joined what one Dutch rider called "The League of Ceiling Starers," riders who couldn't sleep for the uppers coursing round their veins.

The stars mixed amphetamine with painkillers, then took sleeping pills to help at night. They got through the Tour feeling ragged, but they remained in contention. But the proportion was critical. It is probable that overdoing painkillers was what caused Roger Rivière's near-fatal crash in the Tour of 1960, for example.

Rivière, a world-class pursuiter and holder of the world hour record, had attacked on the stage to Lorient in a fit of pique to upset his team-leader, Henry Anglade. French teams were riven by jealousy and personal disputes and Anglade had the equal-opportunities merit of being disliked by everyone. Rivière took 14 minutes out of Anglade in a day, to the delight of the Italian Gastone Nencini, who tagged along with him. It ended Anglade's hope of winning, and lifted Nencini so far up the general classification that he took the yellow jersey instead.

It was bad enough to rob another Frenchman, still worse to give the lead to an Italian. But Rivière had a plan. He figured that if he could follow Nencini over the mountains, he could use his greater speed on the flat to take the yellow jersey from him in the final time trial. It all seemed so easy. Unfortunately, there two other factors. The first was that Nencini was lighter than Rivière, who was built like the typical powerful track rider he was, and therefore a better climber. The other was that Nencini not only went up faster, he could also descend terrifyingly fast, rounding hairpins so dangerously that Raphaël Géminiani said of him that "the only reason to follow Nencini downhill is if you've got a death wish."

Nevertheless, Rivière had to try. He stuffed himself with Palfium, a painkiller, to get him up the climb of the Perjuret and reached the summit fifth, right on Nencini's wheel. Then came the descent, a series of zigzags with a gulf to both sides. Nencini was as faultless as ever, Rivière less lucky. He missed a bend and plunged into a ravine. His teammate Louis Rostollan was the only one to see it happen and came to a hurried halt.

He looked round at the following cars and raised a hand to signify something wrong. He wanted help from anyone, but particularly from an ambulance and from his manager, Marcel Bidot. Radio Tour, though, interpreted the appeal as the sign of a punctured tire, and Bidot arrived without great urgency but with spare tires at hand. He saw Rostollan peering into the valley and assumed he had dropped his useless wheel down the slope. Instead, lying on a grassy bank under trees, there lay Roger Rivière with his back broken. A helicopter lifted him to hospital, turning in the sky "in the manner of a carrion crow," in the words of the French writer Antoine Blondin.

Rivière knew what he had done but was ashamed or reluctant to expose the secret world of professional cyclists and the things they did. Shamelessly, he blamed his broken back on his mechanic, insisting there had been oil on his rims and that his brakes had not worked. The *mécano*, not surprisingly, was outraged. Then word got out: doctors had discovered a stash of tablets in Rivière's jersey and analyzed the massive dose of Palfium in his blood. The man only too willing to blame a hapless mechanic working late into the night on minimum wages had been simply too numb himself to pull his brake levers.

You would think that at the very least that would raise some eyebrows. It stimulated some interest, naturally, and Rivière later sold his story to the papers, confessing that the previous year he had taken drugs to beat the world hour record. "I had to take stimulants for the heart and muscles," he admitted. "Five minutes before the start I had a big injection of amphetamine and solucamphor, and during the attempt I had to take another five tablets because the injections would work for only 40 minutes." Later he admitted being an addict who downed thousands of tablets a year.

Apart from that, though, there was little fuss. There was much disappointment that a great man's career had ended so dreadfully, of course, but little fuss about the route he had taken to cause it to happen. What caused a greater stir was a death that same year in the Olympics. People half knew what was going on in professional cycling — syringes and tin foil along the route were a clue — but the Olympics were for amateurs who worked by day and trained by night to win kitchen clocks and canteens of cutlery.

The 1960 Tour de France ended on July 17, and the Rome Olympics began on September 1, the first Games of what the Olympic movement calls the Modern Era. For most, it was the Games of the extraordinary Australian runner Herb Elliott, who won the 1,500 m in a world record of 3:35.6 and a lead of 20 meters. For those who saw the way things were going beneath the surface, it was the Games of an unknown Danish cyclist, Knud Enemark Jensen.

Jensen was a member of the Danish team in the 100 km time-trial, an Olympic novelty. In a Games at which the Dutch cycling federation chairman Piet van Dijk said "dope — whole cartloads — [were] used in such royal qualities," Jensen began weaving dangerously before collapsing. Doctors took him to the Santa Eugenio hospital, where he died. The autopsy showed that he had taken amphetamine and Ronicol, a drug which dilates the blood vessels. The verdict, because nobody was yet much concerned with drugs in sport, was "sunstroke."

Sixteen years later, Wlodzimierz Golebiewski had a clearer picture. The organizer of the Peace Race [the Eastern Bloc's amateur equivalent of the Tour de France] and Vice-President of the International Amateur Cycling Federation wrote in a work on the history of Olympic cycling: "This young man had taken a large overdose of drugs, which had been the cause of his death. No one has ever proved whether he took the overdose himself or whether the drug was administered by someone else without his knowledge. As a result of this accident, the Union Cycliste Internationale became the first to bring in doping controls."

The initiative came in fact not from the UCI but from the International Sports Medicine Federation. Its spokesman was Pierre Dumas, a Parisian doctor and black-belt judo enthusiast. For most of his life, he had known no more about cycling than he'd read in the papers. Then his name came up in 1952 as a man who could take over the Tour de France medical service at short notice. It was July, and the Tour was only days away, but the offer was so appealing that Dumas canceled a climbing vacation in the Alps and joined the race. He was immediately shocked by the drug-taking going on openly and frequently without any concern about h hygiene. He was alarmed, too, at unqualified men offering powerful drugs and unregulated treatment to their riders. He was powerless to do much but gradually he made his influence felt.

Lucien Aimar, winner of the Tour in 1966, recalled: "Dumas began by making us take tests when I was in the French amateur team in 1962–63. We gave urine samples, and the medications we'd taken were noted. The results were kept a secret, but Dumas used them to find out how to detect all the drugs then in circulation."

Dumas's enthusiasm increased along with his alarm at the scale of the problem. He once intercepted a parcel of amphetamines on its way to a soigneur who had looked after Jacques Anquetil. "I offered to inject him myself, but he refused," he told *L'Équipe*. "I said, 'You're a little shit, you are. It's fine for the other guys but not for you.'"

For Dumas, the death of a rider in an event of such general significance as the Olympics was a sad but valuable opportunity. On behalf of his fellow sports doctors, he demanded that the UCI test riders in the 100 km time-trial in Tokyo in 1964. The UCI could hardly refuse, and riders were told to present themselves for inspection. The first test was simply to look for signs of recent injections. Those who had them were asked what they had taken and who had supplied it. Most cooperated happily.

Teams were then frisked as they came to the start. Urine tests were taken at the finish from the Dutch, Italian, Swedish, Argentinean, Russian, and French teams. They revealed nothing but inoffensive treatments, and they had no legal significance because the Olympics had no anti-doping laws. But Dumas, the four UCI officials, and the French sports minister Maurice Herzog, who between them encouraged or operated the tests, had established the world's first large-scale drugs test.

Herzog — coincidentally in June 1950 the first man to climb the mountain of Annapurna in northern Nepal — was enthused. Dumas had been working on him for a while, insisting that if sport in general, and cycling in particular, wouldn't put their own house in order, it would be necessary for the state to do the job. The result was *la loi Herzog*, published in November 1964 and enacted in July 1965 with just one change: the alteration by the president, Charles de Gaulle, of *le doping* to the more French *le dopage*, the term used in France to this day.

At the same time doctors at the Olympics wrote to the UCI and to Avery Brundage, the Detroit-born millionaire who'd run in the 1912 Games and had become their president 40 years later. They explained how they had proved that tests could be carried out and demanded their general introduction.

Their letter was seen by Prince Alexander de Merode, the pioneering anti-drugs campaigner who died in November 2002, who met Dumas and his Belgian counterpart, André Dirix. They talked for two hours in what was described as a lively conversation, and that same day team doctors from France, Belgium, Holland, Poland, Argentina, Switzerland, the USSR, Iran, the Arab Union, Kenya, Venezuela, Israel, Rhodesia, and Romania signed a petition of support.

It would be a lie to say that most riders appreciated either the change or the law's introduction: they didn't. Riders like Rivière and Jean Mallejac, who'd collapsed on Mont Ventoux in 1955 with his drug-ridden brain still turning his pedals and who "struggled, gesticulated, shouted for his bike, and wanted to escape [from the ambulance] so much that he had to be strapped down," were unfortunate cases who had overdone it a bit, but that didn't mean everyone else deserved censure. As Rudi Altig said, "We are professional cyclists, not athletes."

Not surprisingly, therefore, they reacted strongly when police, drug-testers, and bailiffs descended on the Tour de France in Bordeaux in 1966. Most riders disappeared when word got around. They had seen how things had gone in Belgium, where a law had been passed a few months before France did. Police there had raided changing rooms and riders had sent pills and syringes cascading to the floor rather than be caught with them. They knew it would be just a matter of time before it would happen in France. Rumor said it would be in Bordeaux just before the Pyrenees. And rumor was right.

The Tour's own grapevine worked well. Everyone had vanished by the time the drugs team reached Raymond Poulidor's hotel, and he was the only rider they could find.

## Whatever Happened to... Pierre Dumas

Dr. Pierre Dumas joined the Tour in 1952, an era of "soigneurs, fakirs, who came from the six-day races. Their value was in the contents of their cases, which was their commercial worth...

"...Riders took anything they were given, even bee stings and toad extract. In 1953 and 1954 it was all magic, medicine, and sorcery."

The Tour medical service expanded under Dumas and he was joined in 1972 by Gérard Porte. Dumas retired in 1997, and Porte took over and remains with the Tour to this day. Dumas died in a home for invalids in eastern Paris, aged 78, in February 2000.

"I was strolling down the corridor in ordinary clothes when I came across two guys in plain clothes," he remembered. "They showed me their cards and said to me, 'You're riding the Tour?'

"I said 'Yes.'

"'You're a rider?'

"I said 'Yes.'

"'OK, come with us.'"

It doesn't say much for the police: Poulidor's face had been in every newspaper and magazine in France for years, and yet they hadn't recognized him. Either that or they were being super-formal and refused to be overawed by what was one of the best-loved men in France.

"I swear, it happened just like that," Poulidor said. "They made me go into a room, I pissed into some bottles, and they closed them without sealing them. Then they took my name, my date of birth, without asking for anything to check my identity. I could have been anyone, and they could have done anything they liked with the bottles."

A handful of others, including Rik van Looy, were also found, and some obliged and some refused. All were pretty angry about it. Next morning they rode five kilometers out of the city and stopped in the university area of La House, in the suburb of Gradignan. These days it's where the modern *autoroute* distributes traffic for Paris, Barcelona, and the Mediterranean. There they got off and went on strike, chanting as they walked slowly with their bikes and demanding that Dumas, identified as the cause of their problem, also take a test to see if he'd been drinking wine or taken an aspirin.

The protest had several consequences, though abandoning the dope tests wasn't among them. The first was the Tour's organizers, Jacques Goddet and Félix Lévitan, became convinced that commercial interests were behind the strike and announced that the following year's Tour would be for national rather than sponsored teams. That meant that the Tour would return to the way it had been run from 1930 until 1962, after which it had been by sponsor-teams. The sponsors used to hate the national teams and got it reversed only in 1962 by claiming they would go out of business in tough times if their biggest spectacle of the year continued to be denied them. Well, the organizers decided, the sponsors could either take it or leave it, but the national teams would be back.

The second outcome was that the results of the tests at Bordeaux were suppressed until well after the 1966 Tour had finished, and only then, were the positive results announced. And the third was that an unknown Italian called Tommaso De Pra was thrust into a limelight he had never dreamed of occupying.

Having got the taste for striking, riders held a go-slow the next day as well, on the stage from Bayonne to Pau. The brakes went on at just the moment that De Pra had attacked, which suited the strikers very well. De Pra got ten minutes' lead, although it came down to two when racing resumed after the point had been made, and the ringleaders were able to smirk when Goddet and Lévitan were forced to hand the Yellow Jersey to one of the most inconsequential riders in the race.

Among the protesters at La House was Tom Simpson. Identified subsequently by Dumas as a regular drug-taker, he had been cautious about the strike, saying "It gives publicity to the anti-doping affair that we don't need." He may not have realized it at the time, but he was one of the few to gain from Lévitan's decision to go back to national teams in 1967.

Simpson's position as leader of the Peugeot team had been challenged by Eddy Merckx, the rising Belgian who went on to win five Tours, but Peugeot wouldn't release him from his contract. Finally he had got a promise from Felice Gimondi that he could join his Salvarini team in 1968. But that was on

## What Happened to... the Dope Row?

The strike at Bordeaux continued at the world championship. Rudi Altig of Germany won, improving on his second place to Tom Simpson at San Sebastian the previous year. He and Jacques Anquetil refused to be tested. So did others, including Gianni Motta, Jean Stablinski, and Italo Zilioli. Of the medalists, only third-placed Raymond Poulidor went to see the doctor, dehydrated and uncertain he could oblige. He never found out.

"The commissaires told me, 'It's all of you or none of you.' I was suspended for two weeks. Altig kept his jersey," he said. The UCI didn't know what to do. Eventually, the riders were reinstated pending an appeal and the result stood.

condition that he finish the Tour. At the same time, the agent, Daniel Dousset, was pressing him for better results, so that he could negotiate higher fees for the underpaid rider. Simpson had been World Champion at the end of 1965 but lost much of 1966 due to having broken a leg while skiing. His reputation had dwindled by 1967, and he earned barely enough to stay alive. Something big had to happen if he was going to be able to put some money away to spend the rest of his life in Corsica as he planned.

Few riders British riders were strong enough to be much use to Simpson in a national team — at least one, Arthur Metcalfe, was riding during a break from work — but at least he could be sure of undivided support from them and from the team's manager, a London car-hire salesman called Alec Taylor. Taylor's management style was limited to touring the team's rooms with messages that started "Tom wants…" The riders' tactics were limited to trying to stay with the race.

Dousset had told Simpson that his market value would improve only with a stage win or, better still, a podium place in Paris. And 10 percent of the fees of a rider going down was worth a lot less than 10 percent of a rider on the way up, of course. Dousset had only to lose interest in Simpson as an earner and the rider would be out of a career.

The stage Simpson chose was the 13th, a long ride from Marseille to Mont Ventoux and a rush for the line in Carpentras. The terror that Mont Ventoux created cannot be overestimated. The French novelist and sportswriter Antoine Blondin said of it: "We have seen riders reduced to madness under

## How Many Riders Have Died of Drugs?

The question is impossible to answer because many deaths have been attributed to something else — Simpson's and Jensen's to sunstroke, for instance — or because drug-taking wasn't considered abnormal and may even have been considered medically desirable.

Not surprisingly, therefore, estimates vary. At the start of the anti-dope movement in the 1960s, Dr. Albert Dirix, of the International Olympic Committee medical commission, suggested 30. Against that, Professor Paul Chailley-Bert, of Paris, told a conference in 1965 that there had been more than 1,000.

the effect of the heat or stimulants, some coming back down the hairpins they thought they were climbing, others brandishing their pumps and accusing us of murder."

"Reduced to madness" was just what had happened to Mallejac, who "struggled, gesticulated, shouted for his bike, and (…) had to be strapped down." Simpson would have been aware of that episode, which had become enshrined in popular cycling legend. And he could hardly have been unaware of the doping laws, because he'd taken part in a strike against them. And yet, despite all that, he spent more on just one consignment of drugs during the Tour than his roommate, the weekend pro Colin Lewis, earned on a bike all year.

On July 13 he took many of those drugs, topped up by stolen alcohol to boost the effect — Simpson was implicated in a raid on a bar just before the Ventoux — and a few hundred meters before the top of the mountain he wobbled off his bike, climbed back on, wobbled a little further — and died.

Mallejac, Rivière, and Jensen could all be overlooked. Simpson died on the showcase stage of the biggest bike race in the world. Would things finally have to change?

# 10. Testing Times

Nineteen-sixty-five was the year the Sixties really got going. The Beatles made *Help!* and Paul McCartney wrote *Yesterday.* It was the year that André Courrèges introduced the miniskirt. One era ended when Winston Churchill died on January 24, and another started in February when America began bombing North Vietnam. And another bomb fell when dope tests started in cycling.

The government of Belgium, like that of France, had despaired of cycling sorting out its own problems. On April 2, taking drugs in sport became not just an offence against a token rule in a handbook but a criminal offence in itself. The shock to a sport grown used to its own culture and little outside interference was colossal.

The first thing to do was get rid of the goods. One former Belgian independent, or semi-pro, said: "You'd be laughing about what you were taking, and feeling each other's pockets to laugh at the syringe you could feel there, and suddenly shouts would go up and you'd know the police had arrived.

"Then it would suddenly go quiet because people didn't have time to talk, and in a moment all you could hear was the sound of pills bouncing across the floor, and syringes making that dull thump noise as they fell, because we were all emptying our pockets and cases. It cost a fortune, because there was a real market in this stuff, and you'd spend a lot of your earnings on it, but you didn't dare be caught with any.

"The guys nearest the door were most at risk, and nobody wanted to get changed there, but we soon learned to have supporters outside to shout when they saw the cars arrive. The police would muscle round the room and treat us like animals, but there was always a funny side, because if the pills didn't crunch under their boots, they'd go skidding on them and swear worse than we did."

Riders felt bewilderment, anger, and simple confusion. They thought they were athletes, they said, and now they were being treated as criminals. And, since the law's enactment on 2 April 1965, that's just what a sizeable proportion of them had become: criminals. No fewer than 37.5 percent of the professionals tested came up as lawbreakers — certified drug-users. Almost one in four of the amateurs, too.

| Class | Professional | Semipro | Amateur | Under-19 | Total |
|---|---|---|---|---|---|
| Tested | 102 | 36 | 87 | 29 | 254 |
| Positive | 38 | 5 | 20 | 2 | 65 |
| Negative | 64 | 31 | 67 | 27 | 189 |
| Doped % | 37.5% | 16.5% | 23% | 7% | 25.5% |

The sample bottles were taken to the University of Ghent, in the heartland of Flemish cycling. There they were run through what were then the most up-to-date analyzers by three of Belgium's most experienced testers, men previously more concerned with safe food, illness analysis, and the drug-free state of race horses. Their names — Prof. de Vleeschouwer, Prof. de Schaepdryver, and Dr. Moerman — became a slogan of hatred for riders.

There was as yet little shame in being caught. Many people still saw drug-taking as necessary, something any wise rider would do. Many believed it was healthier to take drugs, that they meant less strain and therefore quicker recuperation. There was no social rejection in being branded a drug-taker, only the inconvenience of not being able to race or having to open your wallet for a fine.

| Year | Total % | Professionals % | Amateurs % |
|---|---|---|---|
| 65 | 25 | 37 | 23 |
| 66 | 20 | 27 | 14 |
| 67 | 8 | - | 14 |
| 68 | 8 | 13 | 7 |
| 69 | 8 | 17 | 8 |
| 70 | 4 | 2 | 5 |

The official view was that the tests made things better. The proportion of positives fell year by year. And that, said optimists and those paid to be optimistic, was a sign that cycling had turned a corner, seen a new light, found a new way. Any cliché you liked, really.

The doctors weren't so sure. André Dirix of the Belgian Cycling Medical Commission, the doctor who worked alongside Pierre Dumas at the Olympics, warned that the year-by-year decline was misleading. "Optimism must be qualified," he said. "Negative results were mainly found in races in which the participants were advised of the tests beforehand, such as classic races and championships. Most of the positive cases were found in small competitions where control was carried out without previous notice."

In other words, the culture hadn't changed at all; where riders thought they would get away with it, they downed drugs as enthusiastically as ever. And if they couldn't do that, they'd switch to drugs they believed the tests couldn't find. And if they could do neither, they could take masking agents — drugs taken simply to confuse the testing machines.

That riders took drugs in the first place is at least understandable. To take further drugs to hide the evidence of the first is just devious. They had moved from the barroom habitué who likes a drink too many to the alcoholic who hides his bottles in a state of denial. Far from the culture changing because riders wanted it to or had been forced to, drug-taking was so ingrained that riders were determined to carry on, come what may.

There were 265 tests in Belgium in 1970, and the drugs that doctors found most were ones they couldn't identify with legal certainty. The testing machines produced graphs. Peaks appeared in predictable places for amphetamine and other drugs, but more and more often, there were peaks in new places, as the machines hit something else. Each time it took weeks to find out what it was. Only then could it be named, the details passed to the Belgian cycling federation, meetings held, and the drug finally banned. In that time, riders had several months, and sometimes longer, to use them and get away it.

By 1970, the testers had five years' experience, but so too had the riders. There were lots of negative tests from championships, classics, and other important races where riders knew there would be a control. There they could ride clean or on undetectable drugs. Those who were caught were stupid, mentally or physically addicted, or just arrogant.

'teriums and other tinpot races, tests were less likely — and that's where most of the positive results were found. On any given day, there were more races than test kits, so the odds were always in the drug-takers' favor, especially if there was a big race elsewhere in the country. The big riders went there, and so did the testers, because of the importance of the race. That meant that most doping, or at least un-clever doping, was at lower levels, among the workaday professionals not worthy of the big teams and, more alarmingly, among those who hadn't reached even that status. Dirix worried that "most of the positive cases were among amateurs, on whom the future of cycling really depends."

|  | Pros | Amateurs | Juniors | Novices | Others | Total |
|---|---|---|---|---|---|---|
| Amphetamine | 1 | 5 | 1 | 1 | 1 | 9 |
| Methyl-amphetamine | 2 | 2 | - | - | 1 | 5 |
| Norephedrine | 2 | 1 | - | - | - | 3 |
| Ephedrine | 5 | 2 | - | 1 | - | 8 |
| Caffeine (not banned) | 1 | 2 | - | - | - | 5 |
| Unknown alkaloids | - | 1 | 3 | - | 1 | 5 |
| Unknown | 4 | 11 | - | 2 | 1 | 18 |

So ingrained was the drug culture that 'the future of cycling' took more unidentifiable drugs than all the forbidden drugs put together. Dirix says they were "probably stimulants," so the official view that doping in Belgian cycling (and by extension anywhere else) had fallen looked no more solid than a house of cards. The enthusiasm for drugs hadn't changed. Only the shape of the problem.

Of course, if you can't go to the control with a clear conscience, the only thing left is not to go to the control, or to trick it. The journalist David Saunders remembered the amateur Milk Race, the Tour of Britain, in 1965:

From my seat in a car just behind the leading group, I saw a Spanish rider urinating as he freewheeled at the back of the breakaway as they rode towards Newcastle on stage 12. There was [sic] just 30 miles to go and the break had just turned on to the A1 [highway] at Rushyford when the Spaniard relieved himself. It was not the action that worried me but a thought that had entered my mind.

There was a popular misconception about hiding the traces of dope by doing this so that when asked to give a sample at the finish nothing would be evident in it, the traces having previously been removed. This was completely untrue, of course, for traces of amphetamine drug could still be found in urine up to 48 hours after taking an artificial stimulant…

This incident, coupled with the testing and another occurrence earlier in the day, had combined to make me feel rather worried about the situation. The earlier matter, taken on its own, had little bearing on things but, in joining it with the other items there seemed to be a somewhat alarming set of circumstances. The first and, then, seemingly unrelated incident occurred when Santamarina of Spain broke away alone as the field began the notorious climb of Rosedale Abbey, sometimes called the Rosedale Chimney, just 25 miles after the Scarborough start.

News of his progress was coming over the Tour radio when a sudden announcement that he had crashed into a car surprised everyone. What had happened was that the Spaniard had ridden straight into the back of one of the official cars parked off the road, waiting to carry out a time check.

The report came back that he had picked himself up laughing, remounted and continued the climb. I remember looking at my colleague and co-announcer, David Duffield, and we just raised our eyebrows and remarked that it was rather strange.

As Santamarina forged steadily ahead to take the overall lead… I must admit to not dismissing the sudden and almost inexplicable crash from my mind. Perhaps I was looking for proof of my own thoughts and when this very fine Spaniard proceeded to water the A1 right in front of my eyes later in the day it seemed that my conclusions were being proved.

It's interesting to note the tone of Saunders' words, as if something the British used to call "not quite cricket" was happening. Which is true, and he was right, but it is hard to imagine the same sniffy tone being taken in more world-weary days. The incident even brought some huffing in the British parliament.

Anyway, Santamarina won the stage and was sent to the drug control, as he knew he would be. So too were two other Spanish riders, Usamentiaga and Canet, and the Briton Ken Hill, who rode for a mixed Midlands-Wales team even though he came from Liverpool, which was in neither. Two days later they were all found positive for amphetamine, Hill claiming he'd been given drugged drinks by other riders, the Spanish that their samples had been mixed up, mistakes made, that they had only taken caffeine. The whole Spanish team went home.

Hill wasn't the last to claim it was others who'd done it. The offence was to take a drug intentionally, not to take one unwittingly. Claim that a bottle had been spiked by another rider or an anonymous spectator, and it was for the law to prove otherwise.

Jock Wadley, the editor of *Sporting Cyclist*, who followed the Tour from 1955 to 1972, said: "It is a defense which stood out a mile to cycling lawyers when they first read the French governmental law 65,412 concerning the repression of stimulants in sporting events."

And such things did happen. Amphetamine was widely available in pep pills and slimming aids. And the enthusiasm of spectators for their favorite riders shouldn't be underestimated. Those were the same fans, remember, who stood guard outside changing rooms to watch for police raids.

Riders saw the sport as a cat-and-mouse of finding new drugs, using them, then abandoning them for something else as the labs were rumbling what was going on.

Dirix said: "It is well known that cyclists informed by ill-intentioned counselors are looking for doping products which are so far unidentifiable in laboratories (…) and the use of hormonal anabolic drugs is expanding in a worrying way and presents a new danger for the health of riders."

Just how cynical things could be was explained in his biography, admittedly unintentionally, by Freddy Maertens. It was all the fault of Belgian officials who led riders to shoot themselves in the foot as well as in the arm, he protested:

> There was always a commotion when a product that until then had been allowed suddenly turned up on the list of banned substances. When a doctor discovered a new product in a urine sample in Italy, all the teams were informed about it. A rider who carried on using it knew that he was making a mistake. In Belgium, however, they did things rather differently. They would keep quiet about a new discovery, let the riders carry on racing, and then out of the blue they would issue a list of the names of the riders who had been

found using it. To me, that is typical of the Belgian federation, which has never failed to do things in a completely underhand way.

To say nothing, of course, of underhand riders prepared to take drugs they expected to get away with.

"Non-observance" was now the only way. Or, put another way, trickery.

Dr. Roland Marlier, of the UCI Medical Commission, said in December 1971:

> We first realized that riders were concealing little bottles about their person when the sample flasks full of urine were stone cold. Since then, riders have not been able to give their sample unless under close observation.
>
> If you think this is a crafty move, then think of the other dodges that have come to light for one reason or another. In the course of testing samples at one race, we appeared to have tested a pregnant woman; on another occasion a professional rider came to cry on my shoulder after being declared positive. He had asked a friend to provide him with a sample, and that friend had been a policeman!

## Whatever Happened to... Freddy Maertens?

Freddy Maertens, aptly described by a Dutch friend as having "a special face" — all uncontrollable lips and hooded eyes — was born on the Belgian coast at Nieuwpoort on 13 February 1952.

His career is one of the more erratic any athlete can have had, winning more than 50 races for two years running (1976 and 1977) and less than half as many in the next three years, followed by a World Championship and eight stages of the Tour, followed by two criterium wins in six years.

He says he earned more than $2,500,000 in prizes alone, let alone contracts, start money, and endorsement deals. The whole lot vanished in unwise investments, and he spent years being pursued by the tax people. He lost his house and moved in with his wife's parents.

He stopped racing in 1987 and has been extensively unemployed since. Raphaël Géminiani observed: "He should have stayed in cycling a lot longer, but he burned the candle at both ends."

The routine for giving a false but warm sample was to attach a flexible rubber bottle to one armpit and run a length of tubing from there to the leg of your shorts. It almost always worked. Most officials were too embarrassed to watch closely and too reluctant to make problems by checking for bottles and tubes. It was even easier for women: no male official, and few female ones, were prepared to follow a woman into a cubicle. She could empty one bottle into another in comfort. The same sensitivity applied to adults checking young boys.

Marlier's assessment of urine samples under "close observation" is therefore pretty fluid. Provided riders appeared to be peeing, that was all that was asked. If that failed, you could go to greater extremes. The journalist Tony Bell told of a rider he knew who, "aware that he had ingested enough amphetamine to keep a thousand dancers going on an all-nighter at Wigan Casino [a well-known disco], he turned to a team-mate for help. The old pro instructed him to find someone to supply a clean sample which he should conceal about his person. Having done this, he was told to go into the test room 'and wait for the diversion.'

"Our man was as startled as the drug test official when a house brick smashed the window, but taking advantage of the ensuing mêlée, he squirted the clean sample into the bottle and survived to race another day."

Doctors could be fans, and as much in awe as ordinary spectators of the stars they were testing, but in the end they weren't to be made fools of. They were not always prepared to look away while a rider fiddled with rubber plumbing that wouldn't work. More and more riders got caught.

| Category | Number examined | Positive | Negative | + % | Non-observance |
|---|---|---|---|---|---|
| Professional | 85 | 2 | 83 | 2.35 | 5 |
| Amateur | 127 | 6 | 121 | 4.72 | 7 |
| Junior | 27 | 1 | 26 | 3.7 | - |
| Novice | 9 | 1 | 8 | 11.11 | 1 |
| Other | 14 | 1 | 13 | 7.14 | - |
| Women | 3 | 0 | 3 | 0 | - |
| Total | 265 | 11 | 254 | 4.15 | 13 |

Eef Dolman, World Amateur Champion on the Nürburgring in Germany in 1966, was disqualified after winning the following year's Dutch Professional Championship when the doctor hauled up his clothing.

"So that's what we're up to, Eef?" he said.

"That's what we're up to," Dolman replied glumly.

That, and money problems, brought his career to an early end. He rode another few years before starting work as an electrical repair man in Dordrecht. He has become introverted, suffers with his health, and has been in hospital with mental problems.

"There's no denying that we took amphetamines in those days; then came the dope controls, and we went from no restrictions to the witch-hunt of the checks— that really shook me," he said.

The Dolman incident prompted officials to insist that riders strip from chest to knees and elbow to wrist. That should have spelled the end for the drug-takers. They'd nab you if you took the stuff, and they'd nab you if you tried to hide it. But why, when so many were caught in two-hour criteriums,

The Tom Simpson memorial on Mont Ventoux, where passing cyclists pay homage with offerings of biking paraphernalia ranging from water bottles to broken bike parts.

were so few riders caught in the three weeks and two mountain ranges of the Tour de France?

Alec Taylor, manager of Tom Simpson's Tour team in 1967, thought he had the answer: "Race officials, federations, even the law on the Continent, [were] lax. I saw the overcautious way riders were tested for dope, as if the authorities feared to lift the veil, scared of how to handle the results, knowing all the time what they would be."

The journalist Jim Manning looked deeper and came to the same conclusion. Despite his reputation as a digger who got to the root of sports stories, he had nevertheless taken a light-hearted view of dope controls. He considered athletes filling glass jars with urine as a jolly thought. But he changed his mind when Simpson died. He started prodding in the records of the hospital at Avignon, where Simpson's autopsy had been carried out. He discovered the truth which nobody had yet found and which the Tour hadn't seen fit to announce: that, in his words, Simpson was so drugged that he "no longer knew what he was doing."

But why hadn't the French said so? It was their law, their crime, their police, their doctors.

"Is France trying to hush up the scandals of the Tour?" he demanded in the London *Daily Mail*, and continued:

> I say yes. The first act of hushing up is not to attempt detection, let alone waiting for a year before taking action. How much husher can you get?
>
> Three days after this year's race, the French authorities announced that *next October and November* a French and an Italian rider would be prosecuted for alleged doping offences in last year's Tour. France had surrendered the need rigorously to prevent doping, to the discreet requirement of not tackling it on a big tourist occasion until a year had passed safely.

| Riders tested | 139 |
|---|---|
| Amphetamine | 5 |
| Ephedrine | 6 |
| Strychnine | 2 |
| Other alkaloids | 17 |

Test results, 1967 World Championships, Holland.

That is my accusation. I nail it firmly to the wall. It takes two days at most to analyze samples; it took a year for France to authorise prosecutions. What devious explanations can be expected?

Not that that provided a lesson even for British riders. Less than a month after Simpson died, Roger Newton came second in the British Professional Championship with the help of a dose of amphetamine. He blamed a vitamin pill bought in Switzerland. He was followed by Albert Hitchen in the Tour of the

## Whatever Happened to... the Simpson Affair?

The answer is nothing, beyond a memorial on Mont Ventoux. Britain held no inquiry into his death. There was no inquest in Britain because he'd died abroad. There was no inquiry beyond the autopsy in France because he was British and lived in Belgium. And there was no action by the British Cycling Federation because of the pandemonium. By chance, the man in charge of the three-room office, Len Unwin, was on vacation when the news broke. That left the racing secretary, Bryan Wotton, to handle the thousands of inquiries.

When I asked years later if there had been any inquiry into why a rider in a Great Britain jersey had dropped dead in the world's biggest race, he confessed the idea had never occurred to him. Not, he said, because there shouldn't have been one, but by the time the world had stopped pouring in on his little office near Regent's Park, the sport in Britain was more in mourning than looking for scapegoats.

Jacques Anquetil blamed Simpson's death not on taking amphetamines but on not taking enough. Simpson had had to be cautious, he said, because of the tests that could lie ahead and yet, with astonishing mental flexibility, he then claimed Simpson should have been given still more amphetamine on the mountainside to kick-start his heart into action.

Lucien Aimar, who caught Simpson on Mont Ventoux, insisted: "They made an emblem of him. The result of pushing Simpson and the problem of amphetamines to the forefront was the tightening of dope controls and riders were pushed toward more and more dangerous medicaments."

West, also drugged with amphetamine, and by Martin Filmer, who refused to take a test.

UCI secretary René Chésal nevertheless saw hope and change. Of August's World Championships in Holland he said: 'This will be the first guaranteed dope-free world cycling championships, of that we can be sure.' Or not so sure. The championships hadn't reached their first Saturday evening before Yvonne Reynders and Alex Boeye of Belgium, Dieter Kemper of Germany, Freddy Ruegg of Switzerland, and Kevin Crowe of Australia had all been flung out for taking drugs.

André Dirix said: "It was in those championships that we found positives for ibogaine, a substance virtually unknown in medical circles and composed of three alkaloids (...) from an extract of shrubs found in the Far East and used for centuries by native hunters to keep them awake. So at the same time we're seeing a return to old medicines of plant extracts and a search for products practically unknown by laboratories. 'Advisers' deliberately look for new products which metabolite analysis can't yet detect."

The Pan-American Games at Winnipeg, Canada, were hardly cleaner. Eight of the 57 riders tested were positive, five for methyl amphetamine, three for amphetamine.

That fall ( 1967), Britain held its first six-day race for decades. Two of the riders engaged for London, Ron Baensch and Leandro Faggin, were proved drug- takers. Another, Tom Simpson, was obviously no longer there to ride.

"There'll be no dope used in the race, you can be sure of that," promised the flamboyant Dutch organizer Charles Ruys, whose unusual administrative techniques ensured he wasn't asked back another year. "If any rider uses it, he'll be out of the race straight away, although we don't want lots of publicity about it."

I'll leave you to solve the contradiction of being willing to throw international riders out of the country's biggest track event in decades and the reluctance to have lots of publicity about it. Of Baensch and Faggin he said: "As far as I'm concerned, they've paid their penalty already."

Later he explained the rigorous nature of his checks: He had gone through the riders' bags, he said. "I noticed one rider on the fourth night was going particularly well. I was through his bags before he had finished and got back to his cabin. There wasn't even a trace of anything suspect." André Dirix must have wondered why he'd gone to all the expense of elaborate testing machinery...

Elsewhere on the track, Jacques Anquetil was denied his World Hour record after refusing a test in the track center. He refused Dr. Giuliano Marena's demand that he fill a bottle in a makeshift cabin within sight of thousands of spectators at the Vigorelli track, saying he should be allowed the dignity of giving the sample at his hotel. A scuffle followed, and the doctor waited two hours at the track but went home when Anquetil didn't return.

Anquetil gave a sample to a French doctor when he got back to Rouen and said the rules allowed him 48 hours and that the sample was still valid. But the UCI said it wasn't and Anquetil lost his record. Shortly afterwards he said, "Yes, I had taken something, but not what those *messieurs* were looking for." The *messieurs* carries more sarcasm than the straight translation of "gentlemen." Anquetil's career was never the same afterwards.

September 1967, just two months after Simpson's death, a 25-year-old Belgian professional called Roger De Wilde began zigzagging and crashed while he was leading a criterium with three others at Kemzeke in Belgium. The police examined his bike and said there was nothing wrong with it. Doctors found he had taken amphetamine, and *L'Équipe* reported that he had had a heart attack as a result. Shortly afterwards, three riders — Noel de Pauw, André Messalis and Willy Bocklandt — were fined, and De Pauw and Messalis given suspended jail sentences for taking drugs in the Tour of Flanders.

They defended themselves by saying "All cyclists take drugs." The judge, Pierre Dhaenens, didn't accept the justification.

# 11. Bucking The System

After Simpson's death in 1967 it became clear that things had to change in the Tour de France. The organizers had wanted a fresh start with national teams and the idea had been generally welcomed. The riders had no experience with it and spent much of the race trying to work out who was supposed to be riding for whom and how, but for spectators there was something they could understand.

Continental enthusiasts grasp perfectly well the notion of riders from different countries grouping together to ride under the name of a refrigerator maker or, these days, even moneylenders. But nothing beats some sort of personal identity, personal allegiance, which is why in other sports equally rootless teams compete in the names of their cities or regions: the Pittsburgh Pirates, Manchester United, Paris St.-Germain. Most of the players don't come from those places but it's much more satisfying to shout for something you recognize.

As long-time Tour reporter Geoffrey Nicholson said: "It's much easier to shout *Allez France* than *Allez Mercier-BP.*"

I doubt whether anybody realized it at the time, but Simpson's death could be at least loosely associated with the return to national teams. Even if it had, it wouldn't be enough to change the Tour organizer's underlying desire to stick up a finger in the face of stroppy sponsors whom were seen as getting above themselves.

The 1968 Tour, therefore, remained for national teams, as it had been in 1967, but there would be a further change in the light of 1967 Mont Ventoux tragedy: This would be a "Tour of Health." It would start at Vittel, a town not much known outside France, but well-known within the country as the source of endless bottles of spa water. What better way to emphasize a race "on mineral water"— as clean as the winter snows that fed the springs of northeast France?

Tactfully, the Tour also removed Mont Ventoux, shortened many of the stages, and held 11 stages before any mountains were reached at all.

The race ran repeatedly afoul of its schedule, either because riders weren't "dipping their nose in the bag," as Pierre Dumas used to put it, or more likely because of day-after-day of head winds and because an unusually large number of teams had good sprinters and blocked the race to keep them fresh for the finish. Bizarrely, people began reminiscing about the "good old" days when riders could take however long it took them.

What was supposed to be a bright new beginning turned into what journalists began calling the "Tour of Boredom." Félix Lévitan was furious and accused them during a television interview with being blasé and of "watching with tired eyes." The entertaining outcome was that the reporters went on strike, ironically on the way to Bayonne, which had produced the riders' strike two years earlier and led to the whole situation in the first place. Instead of watching the race with notebooks, cameras, and microphones in hand, they sat by the roadside in the dark glasses of the blind and jeered Lévitan as he passed. He smiled back cynically.

Raymond Poulidor saluted with a clenched fist, which some saw as a threat and others as a sign of solidarity. Other riders waved as they spotted banners warning, "Riders! You are being watched with tired eyes." Pierre Dumas, who had caused so much of the change, observed drily, "*Ah, la Sorbonne des vélos...*"

The Sorbonne is Paris's prestigious university, and that year the focus of a year of strikes and street-fighting across France. "*Les événements de 68*" had no clear aim except to change the status quo, especially in education, and in a more general way to change the stuffy, patriarchal way in which France was run. Nine million people joined a general strike, cobbles were hurled, and protesters and policemen killed. The government faltered, and Charles de Gaulle dissolved parliament. Things came to an end only after thousands poured into the Champs Élysees and demanded a return to normal.

Dumas's reference to "*la Sorbonne des vélos*" was a beautifully pointed reference to a lot of fuss with no clear purpose while at the same time insulting the journalists with the ironic reference to a university.

When the reporters went back to work, they could report that there had been just two positive drug tests, including the oldest man in the race, Jean Stablinski. A year earlier, throwing out a *grand patron* and former national champion would have caused uproar. Now the atmosphere had changed enough that nobody wept. Indeed, just two positive results from 110 starters, 63 finishers, and 23 stages was indeed another sign of a fresh start, new horizons, etc. The "Tour of Health" may have been dull, but it showed that racing around France on Vittel water for a month was possible.

Or perhaps it was not quite so positive after all. Looking back just before his death, the Tour organizer, Jacques Goddet, confessed in December 1999: "The controls we developed after Simpson's death were a lie, covered up by the highest scientific and medical authorities, and I condemn them."

It was a shame he didn't make more of it at the time, but at least there was now official confirmation: riders hadn't changed their ideas about drug-taking, the "lie" of the dope controls was contrived, according to Goddet, to maintain those ideas; and riders were clearly largely unafraid of the tests they were asked to go through from the "Tour of Health" onwards.

Just how unafraid became obvious on Alpe d'Huez in 1978. That was 13 years after the start of regular dope-testing, and 11 years after Simpson's death and Dolman's trickery. The Belgian national champion, a balding 27-year-old called Michel Pollentier, was in the polkadot jersey of best climber as the race left the former bike-making city of St.-Étienne for the 240 km stage to Alpe d'Huez. It was a long day with a tough finish, an epic finish at the top of a series of hairpins lined by thousands of fans.

Normally the mountains leader would be allowed little scope, but that year and that day, Bernard Hinault, the eventual winner, was much more concerned with his immediate rival, Joop Zoetemelk. Each looked at the other and waited for a reaction when Pollentier, as ugly on his bike as he was pleasant off it, attacked on the climb of Chamrousse. And since neither Hinault nor Zoetemelk was prepared to help the other by starting a chase, the little Belgian crabbed and pumped his way to a three-minute lead.

He still had two minutes at the foot of the hairpin climb to the finish, Hinault and Zoetemelk now finally chasing. For a wearer of the polkadot jersey, Pollentier was in fact not a world-class climber. He lost time as he twisted and grimaced to the top of the mountain but he still had 37 seconds on Hennie Kuiper, who had waited for the race leaders to react and then profited from it, 45 seconds on Hinault and 1:18 on Zoetemelk, who had cracked on the climb.

It was a glorious moment for the little Belgian, changing the red and white of the *bolletjes* (little balls) jersey, as it is known in Belgium, for the prestige of the *maillot jaune*. Now this wasn't the way to ride if you're afraid of the dope test. The way to ride if you are afraid of the dope test is to hide yourself away in the bunch, finish outside the first ten, and pray that your name doesn't come up in the random selection for testing.

Pollentier, on the other hand, felt so sure that he would get away with the same trick as Dolman — after a decade of having to "strip from chest to knees and from elbow to wrist" — that he turned up at the test center with the same contraption of bottles and pipes. And not only he, but one of the other two riders called as well. The doctor, the Italian Renaldo Sacconi, grew suspicious, first of the Frenchman Antoine Guttierez, and then tugged up Pollentier's jersey to expose him as well.

Pollentier had been so confident of his ability to cheat the control, that he had drugged himself with amphetamine, by then an obvious and unsophisti-

## How Are Riders Picked for Dope Controls?

The British Milk Race was possibly the first big stage race to have daily tests. There were inevitable gaps in the procedure which experience revealed only later. There was no formal witnessing of samples, no formal way of picking riders to be tested.

Checks were random, any six riders a day. That seemed all-embracing but it makes for only a one-in-nine chance of being picked. And since some riders would be called more than once, any one rider's chance of being caught on any one day was lower.

The Tour de l'Avenir, the amateur Tour de France, started picking the first three on the day, the first three overall, and several more at random. Lower-placed riders still had a better chance of getting away, but anyone with serious aspirations could expect tests all the time.

cated drug, and ridden off the front to win alone. If Pollentier had tried and been caught, then how many other riders had been equally confident and got away with it? Is that what Goddet meant when he talked of a "lie covered up by the highest scientific and medical authorities?"

Pollentier stood on a hotel balcony later and announced that he had taken something "for his breathing." It was allowed in Italy, he said, but he did not know whether the UCI allowed it, so he thought he would play it safe by tricking the control. Uncertainty? With amphetamine? Amphetamine was the drug that the police in Pollentier's Belgium had been looking for since 1965.

Pollentier then added that at least half the rest of the racers were also using "products." Sensation followed sensation, especially in a world of intense professional secrecy. Pressed, he backtracked and said: "I'm not saying what they are using are drugs." Which makes you wonder why he mentioned it. He also said that other controls in the Tour had been more lenient — presumably no jerseys had been tugged up — and that even so at least one rider had contrived to come third rather than first or second because only the winner and runner-up were tested as a routine.

There was, of course, huge speculation about why the more "lenient" controls had suddenly become tighter for Pollentier and Guttierez. The first rumor was that Renaldo Sacconi was a stickler for rules. And then conspiracy theorists started suggesting that someone within the Tour de France itself had

## Whatever Happened to... Michel Pollentier?

The balding, round-faced and likeable Belgian was fined 5,000 Swiss francs — worth $8,250 in 2002 —, disqualified from the Tour, and suspended for two months (which meant further loss in missed earnings).

He became depressed and sought treatment from a doctor in Ostend on the Belgian coast, under whose care he remained for a year. He had a brief revival and won the Tour of Flanders in 1980, but the flair had gone and he stopped racing on 8 October 1984.

He had lost much of his money through unwise investments and went into business selling car tires. He is still involved in cycling, coaching young riders in Flanders.

objected to a Belgian wearing the yellow jersey at the end of an epic stage and wanted him out.

The first, for all it matters, may be true. Just about the only thing you ask of officials is that they're sticklers for the rules. If not, why have rules and why have officials? The second is ridiculous. It was not as if Belgians had never been in the yellow jersey before. And it's not likely even the French were willing to ruin the Tour's reputation just to see a Frenchman in yellow.

Which leads to a further rumor, that he was set up because he was a threat to Bernard Hinault. This theory, equally unproven, suggests that the doctor was tipped off not by someone in the Tour organization, but by someone else who wanted Hinault to win and not Pollentier. Of all the conspiracy theories, this one was by far the best, because in a nation of 60 million, the vast majority would have preferred Hinault to win. It could have been anybody from the president downward.

The conspiracy theory rests, however, on the idea that Pollentier could have won the Tour. The man was a hard rider, "the last of the real stone-hard characters of Flanders" as Rik van Steenbergen put it. But a winner? The best he'd ever finished was seventh, in 1974 and 1976. He'd never otherwise reached the first 20, and for four of the eight years he rode he didn't even finish.

So who, then? Infuriatingly, those who presumably know won't tell. Pollentier's close friend Freddy Maertens said that Pollentier was set up "from within his own camp," without giving details. And the writer Roger-Pierre Turine insists: "That day, believe me, Pollentier was sold in the way that slaves used to be sold." But again without names.

I called in on Pollentier long after he had left the sport in October 1984, a retirement prompted by mental gloom and hospital treatment. We sat in his front room with a tray of coffee on a low table and a few mementoes of his career on the walls and shelves. He talked happily about whatever I asked, but he gave the impression of having written the incident out of his life. What, as he wrote to Goddet and Lévitan, "should have been the happiest day of my life [but] will be the saddest," was all a long time ago, he said.

He had been warmed to receive "thousands of letters" of support and to be cheered when he went to races in Belgium during his retirement. But what had happened, who if anyone had set him up... It was no longer worth discussing, he said.

# 12. Ingrained in the System

"It's not drugs that makes champions," Erwann Menthéour told the radio station Europe 1 in January 1998. "We'd ride 5 km/h slower if there weren't any, but the same riders would be in front." Arthur Metcalfe, the part-timer who rode at Simpson's side, said a few weeks before his death in 2002: "Perhaps everyone would ride 5 km/h slower. But who would notice that at the roadside? It would be just as hard for the riders, the spectacle would be the same, and you'd have a clean race. Instead, the decision has been to make the stages far shorter than they were in those days, but that just makes them all the faster."

But doping is ingrained, and has been for decades. Vin Denson, another member of that fated 1967 Tour team, recalls traveling to races with Anquetil and another French rider:

> We stopped for lunch and one of the others got out a little metal box and helped himself to some of his amphetamine, just for the thrill. They both had some, emptying the box, but there were some little broken bits and powder left at the bottom. The other guy said it'd be a shame to waste it and so he and Jacques looked around and they saw a fish tank in the corner with these enormous fat fish swimming about. So they got up and tipped the remains of the drugs box into the water and the big old fish saw the stuff settling down on the surface of the water.
>
> Obviously they thought it was food and they swam up to the top and went whoomph and took the whole lot down in one gulp. We all watched to see

what would happen. At first nothing at all happened. And then all of a sudden these fish began thrashing round their tanks like motorboats. Going berserk they were. It was one of the funniest things we'd ever seen.

Note the casual way in which the riders took amphetamine socially and not just for races. This was the stuff kids were taking for wild nights out. If it seemed pretty good to them, it felt just as good for bike riders, whether they were racing or not.

Menthéour remembers going to a disco after riding a criterium on the Côte d'Azur. In the party were a number of riders who had that day finished their careers. Nobody held back with the celebrations, and the night grew wilder and wilder. "One of the rider's wives helped herself to some of her husband's drugs and treated us to a memorable striptease. We joked and laughed all night. At that, at any rate, I can always lead the peloton..."

On another occasion, before a race, he recalled: "When we got there, seven or eight of us riders went into a room and I treated them all. Amphetamines are like aperitifs, a social ritual. You soon dismiss people who take without ever standing their round in turn."

Or take the word of Willy Voet, the soigneur at the heart of the Festina scandal in 1998: "I often used to join two big Belgian riders in the great saga of the post-Tour criteriums. We shared the same car for three weeks, and in that time everything was allowed, all experiences permitted. The most explosive cocktails!"

Menthéour — an educated man, whose love of reading, ability with languages, and skill on the piano marked him out as an intellectual to be disliked by other riders — remembers driving through Belgium and seeing the motorway lights left on all night, in contrast to the darkness of French highways.

"Look," he told his companion, "even the roads are lit up in Belgium."

"Lit up" was a reference to drug-taking, riders referring to a doped rider as "having his headlights on."

He described a start-of-season team presentation as another illustration of how widespread drug-taking was both on and off the bike. The team had gone into the venue's changing room to switch from the clothes in which they'd arrived to first their suits and then, for the benefit of photographers seeing the new colors for the first time, their race clothes.

"Everybody knows that three-quarters of the riders at these official presentations are charged up on amphetamines," he said. "Just look at the group photos and you'll understand what lies behind those laughing faces." The team giggled away in their overexcited way as they heard their sponsor's representative telling the gathering that he condemned doping and that he promised his team would be riding clean.

Menthéour wondered what the bigwig would give to know — or perhaps not to know — "that at the very moment, in the changing rooms, some of his good examples were getting their heads lit up."

Well-meaning words like that are common at presentations and often die within the moment. But this time, said Menthéour, the team got the shock of hearing their *patron* taking an unprecedented step further. Not only would his team ride clean for the sake of the sport and athletic purity, they would do it as part of a campaign against drug-taking in the suburbs and the hopeless streets of the inner cities. His team would be an example, a model, for the youth of the country, he said. They needed guidance — heroes they could respect, and his team would provide them.

A horrified silence fell over the changing rooms. The guy seemed to mean it. He wasn't just mouthing measly mottoes and keeping his fingers crossed behind his back to minimize the lie. The team was horror-stricken, Menthéour said. Until that moment they were going to dope themselves "to death, like every year," because that was the only way they knew to ride bike races.

The most popular way to do it when there are no controls is *pot belge*, a cocktail of almost every drug on earth but specifically cocaine, amphetamine, caffeine, heroin, and sometimes corticoids. It's a colorless liquid in a 10, 15, or less usually a 20 ml bottle. Push a hypodermic through the rubber stopper, draw off a milliliter, and inject it and you're set up. A milliliter is "a million" in bike slang and if you hear riders saying *"un million, un million,"* they're imitating the TV show *Qui veut gagner des Millions?* (Who Wants To Be A Millionaire?) and pointing out a rider "who feels good enough to mow the lawn all night," as Voet describes it.

One bottle will provide enough *lichettes* ("slices," or doses) to last most riders a season. So much is in circulation that even those who never straddle a bike have felt happy to help themselves. Voet remembers a celebration after a major championship, a party which included riders, selectors, and national officials: "Most of the people there injected themselves with a sample of *pot belge* to have a party and to last the night," he recalled. Among them was a rider "baptised" into the world of doping, in Voet's word, after never having taken amphetamines.

Voet then had to drive a rider to the airport at four in the morning and go on afterwards to his own house, "which would be 20 hours of driving after a sleepless night. I didn't want to fall asleep at the wheel, so I had an injection of amphetamine every four hours." Ah yes, he said, he well remembered his time with that team and the party it held.

Voet remembers kitting up a rider to defraud a dope control in 1984. The bottle-under-the-arm trick had died of shame after the Pollentier fiasco, and the new way was to fill a condom with someone else's urine, push it up a rider's backside and run a hair-covered plastic tube under the crotch. All the rider had to do was take care how he walked to the control and then clench his buttocks to give the impression of urinating. It worked faultlessly so many times, Voet said, that he used to buy the plastic tubes wholesale at the start of each season.

The rider that day took the test, happy to know he wouldn't be caught for the drugs he had used, only to get a letter saying he'd been found positive for drugs he knew he *hadn't* taken. What he had taken was ephedrine for his

## Whatever Happened to... Open Drug-Taking?

In the old days, before drug-testing, you could follow the route of the previous weekend's race by the trail of needles and pill-wrappers. Riders who injected themselves openly and had to be pushed off their bikes for their own safety — as happened in the Tour de l'Avenir — were unlikely to fret about the evidence blowing back past the following officials.

Television changed all that when it came to the Tour in 1958 and especially in the following decade, when cameras began watching riders close-up from the pillion of motorbikes. Then, said the Dutch rider Theo Koomen, some riders sewed shortened hypodermics into the small pocket popular at the time in the back of their shorts. A gentle push pressed the needle into their buttocks. Pills and ampules were hidden in the hems of caps, under handlebar tape and even in holes in oranges and apples.

breathing and for the stimulation; what the UCI told him that it had found was Stimul.

There was much gnashing of teeth and tugging of hair. The rider could do nothing but sit out the suspension, which seemed fair enough since he had taken something. But who was it who had supplied the urine, and why was it drug-ridden? It didn't take long to find the answer. The sample had been from one of the mechanics.

"To stay awake at the wheel of his van," Voet said, "he had taken a charge [doped himself]." Ever since, Voet said, the absent-minded mechanic "has thought carefully before opening his tap [supplying urine]."

Stimul is an everyday amphetamine, popular in criteriums and Six Day races. It is exactly the kind of drug that Charles Ruys had made such a fuss of looking for when he claimed to disprove the use of doping by making his search of a single bag at the London Six Day race. One of the most popular riders in that series was a ginger-haired Londoner called Tony Gowland, who progressed from riding the amateur event as a novice in 1967 to winning the professional race with the help of Patrick Sercu.

One night Gowland had hurried from his curtained trackside cabin so as not to delay the fast-moving program. When he came back, one of the experienced Continental riders pulled him to one side and pointed out the drinking bottle that Gowland had left unattended in his rush.

"Take a hint," he said. "Never leave your drinks out like that."

Gowland looked at him puzzled.

"Someone could put something like Stimul in it," the man said.

Gowland assumed he meant as a trick to make him fail any dope test, but the idea of a test hadn't crossed the old pro's mind.

"They'll dose your drink with it and you won't be able to sleep tonight and then you'll lose the race."

If you think that sounds devious, then take the warning of Erwann Menthéour, who says that soigneurs with the power to make you go faster also have the doses to make you go slower. Not only will the less scrupulous try their new drugs on naive riders who trust them, he says, but they are not beyond settling a row by giving a rider a charge of something to slow him down.

# 13. Supply and Demand

P*ot belge* is "the atomic bomb of doping" according to Erwann Menthéour, a drug that riders adore because "efficacy is guaranteed." It's as easy as hell to find in drug tests, of course, but why worry about tests when there aren't any, or when you can cheat the ones that there are?

A single small dose can start at between $85 and $150, he says. It's traded like any other drug, by dealers who hang about at bike races. The profit isn't as high as with heroin but there's none of that inconvenience of having to push it in half-lit back streets and tenement stairways. Not everyone is a buyer, but it's a willing market with new riders always coming in at the bottom and old hands clinging to their fading glory at the top.

At first, Menthéour says, the dealer starts with little presents or introductory prices. The rider takes what he wants for himself and sells the rest for the price he gave the dealer in the first place. That gives him the money to go back to the dealer or, if he prefers to take his profit in kind, a stash of alternative drugs. These in turn he can sell. Each stage adds to the price, which makes it harder to sell, but before long there are doses of *pot belge* circulating at up to $400, Menthéour says.

Two things then happen. The first is that riders find they have moved from simple drug-takers to actual drug dealers. That's why those who wring their hands at the state of the problem so often cite "older riders with old ideas." The other thing that happens is that some riders become hooked, effectively cocaine and heroin addicts. And then the price goes up, as in all drugs markets, but not as severely as on the streets, because the supply is too plentiful.

The other big drug of the moment is erythropoietin — Epogen or EPO — which in hefty doses will make your blood soak up more oxygen than the body ever thought possible. It's like putting a jet engine on a moped.

Its medical use is to produce red blood cells in people, especially children, with anaemia. The attractive angle for both doctors and drug cheats is that it does what the body does for itself — but more so, and so for more than a decade the testers were at a loss how to establish whether the substance had been used by a rider.

Laurent Fignon, winner of the Tour in 1983 and 1984, says: "EPO was around from 1990, but it was hyper-confidential, limited to a little circle of riders. It wasn't yet normalized, used in an organized way as it is now."

Organized so that, as Luc Leblanc put it: "It breaks your heart to see riders storming over high mountains these days, when you knew them two years ago and they had trouble getting over a railway bridge."

EPO is made by Amgen, a world-wide company based in Thousand Oaks, California. You can be sure that it does not get shipped out to just any bike team that asks for it. In fact the company is embarrassed by the way EPO and similar drugs have been used and has helped the World Anti-Doping Agency find a test to detect it. So if Amgen won't sell it to you, where does it come from so plentifully that for a decade it has been "normalized," as Fignon described it? Where, indeed, where do any of these drugs come from?

A good place to start is *L'Équipe Magazine* of September 1998. It's published with the respected sports paper *L'Équipe*, France's biggest-selling newspaper, the biggest sports paper in the world, and stablemate to the Tour de France in the Amaury Sport organization.

The magazine's inquiries revealed a curious difference between the health of Frenchmen and of Italians across the border. You'd expect neighboring western nations to be similar. But cross into Italy, and you're entering the land of the walking sick.

In France only doctors can write prescriptions for EPO, and they consider it appropriate in 3,000 cases a year, mainly cancer sufferers. Italians on the other hand get through 40,000 doses. In France, the drug comes only through hospital pharmacies; in Italy, any family doctor can offer a syringe for $75, much of which will be reimbursed by the state medical service.

Unless Italians are ten times more ill than the French or that all that surplus EPO is thrown down drains — neither of which are hardly credible — it probably goes into a black market, and much of that not just for strictly medical use.

On top of that, huge quantities of copycat EPO, of *pot belge*, and of other drugs are made in former Iron Curtain countries where attitudes to Western patents are more flexible. The method is described on the Internet, and the greatest expense is a carbon-dioxide heater costing $2,500. The ingredients, certain bacteria, are harder to get but the method is easy for any skilled chemist.

This Eastern link was revealed when police questioned a doctor of the Dutch TVM team in July 1998. TVM had been implicated on 9 March 1998, when customs men found 104 doses of EPO in one of the team's cars at a toll station near Reims. What interested police was that one of TVM's doctors was Andrei Mikhailov, a Russian. The net spread from there, Mikhailov having received a $10,000 fine and a suspended jail sentence of 12 months.

A raid on four traffickers in the port city of Marseille in November that same year turned up 4,000 steroid pills, all in boxes labeled in Russian. One of those charged identified himself as a chemist from the Ukraine. Gilles Aubry, deputy director of the French agency responsible for pursuing drug traffickers, reckons 80 percent of amphetamine comes from Poland and Holland and identifies Poland as the source of *pot belge*.

"It keeps happening," Aubry says. "People from the countries of the East are implicated every time. It's a real mafia."

Another source is losses from hospitals. Insiders say that doctors and suppliers worry about disappearing drugs in relation to their value and dangers. That may not be encouraging, but in a practical world it's worse to lose an expensive and dangerous drug than a few boxes of aspirin.

Dr. Alain Duvallet, regional head of the Ministry of Sport and Youth in Paris, estimates the loss of hormones between laboratory and distributor to be 10 to 20 percent, figures "which don't alarm the manufacturer and which fall in the margin of quality control." There are more losses between the wholesaler and the patient, hard to calculate, but estimated at a further three to five percent.

Look for drugs rejected by quality control, or stolen during production or distribution, and you have your supply. If you're not fussy about quality, it's easy. And many people aren't. Hospitals dispose of outdated drugs in wholesale quantities, and there are always those who see value in other people's junk.

In December 1998, the hospital at Aix-en-Provence reported that thieves had robbed its disposal bins of 50,000 doses of EPO. Stocktakers checked supplies that hadn't become outdated and, matching invoices to stocks, found that no fewer than 500,000 doses — ten times as much — had vanished in the preceding months.

Current EPO is of excellent quality. But any bike rider willing to take drugs whose after-effects are unknown in the quantities in which he takes them isn't going to worry about an out-of-date "sell-by" on the packet — assuming he even knows.

If you don't want to go for stolen goods, you can get the real stuff from the Internet. Just tap in the name of what you want, stand by to plough through several thousand offered pages, and you may well get to what you want. You may not be dealing with the kind of person to whom you'd readily trust your credit card number, but then again what's a credit card number to worry about compared to the risk of the drugs?

Much more respectable is to get your supplies from a doctor. An inquiry in 1997 by Patrick Laure, a lecturer at Nancy University and a medical researcher, brought him into contact with 2,000 French athletes pursuing different sports aged 17 or more. Of those who confessed to drug-taking, 61 percent said they had got their supplies during a routine consultation with their doctor, usually by faking a sickness or an injury. Of the rest, 20 percent bought on the black market (including recreational drugs such as cannabis) and most of the rest were supplied by their clubs, their trainers, friends, or parents.

Doctors' prescriptions put sports officials in a difficult position. They can scarcely claim greater knowledge than a doctor. Nor can they safely insist a rider abandons his treatment for the duration of a race, still less throughout the season. They are not keen to face the consequences of a rider dying because they had stopped him from taking his legitimately prescribed medicine. Nor do they fancy being sued by a professional athlete worth millions and with a legal team behind him, an athlete who insists he has the right to work and who maintains that officials are denying him his earnings. If you doubt how vulnerable sports federations can be, just ask the people who used to run British athletics: they were put out of business by a single protest against a positive dope test.

Cynics sneered when the Dutch soigneur Piet Liebregts blamed the authentic medical profession their disdain for medically unqualified soigneurs.

The drugs situation worsened, Liebregts said, when "doctors came on the scene. They went to riders telling them to take this, or that's good (...) That was especially the case in Belgium. If a doctor had two or three racing bikes outside his door, in no time his practice had grown 40 percent." Riders knew nothing of doping before 1960, he said. By which he meant that they knew what was happening but that they trusted their soigneurs. And soigneurs "took great care to see the doses of stimulant were not too much; they took the responsibility."

But years later Liebregts' view was confirmed by none other than Prince Alexandre de Mérode, the president of the Olympic Medical Commission, who worked with Pierre Dumas on the early fight against drugs in the wake of the 1960 Olympics. Doctors, he said, "are in the front row of responsibility. They know what they're up to. It's their prescriptions that make trafficking possible."

In 1979, Joop Zoetemelk said the illegal Nandrolone he'd been caught taking during the Tour de France had been prescribed by his doctor. And that was decades before the same drug began turning up in athletics, where weeping athletes said it "must" have been in their energy food. By 2000, forty percent of riders in the Tour had registered their drugs with UCI doctors. The logic of that was that dozens of the world's healthiest men were riding the Tour hobbling to Paris with sick-notes. Or, looked at another way, 40 percent of the field was so ill that it couldn't ride the race without drugs — drugs that were on the banned list or otherwise there had be no point in declaring them.

"I need it for a medical condition" is a claim that goes back to the start of testing. You would think they could come up with something more original. The difference now is that fear of legal consequences means that riders can make this excuse well before they're caught. And if you didn't need the medication before the race, you can always change your mind afterward.

A doctor speaking at a drugs inquiry in France said: "In regional races you can get a rider who tests positive and then he presents a backdated certificate that he gets from his doctor."

Patrick Béon, former team-mate of Bernard Thévenet and winner of the Étoile de Bessèges in 1975 and the Critérium International in 1976, told a drugs trial in Rennes in 2002: "I was the best amateur of my generation at the start of the 1970s, without taking a single thing. I missed out when I turned pro for Peugeot, though. Riders that I had beaten easily as an amateur were dropping me easily. I took amphetamine, like everybody, for criteriums that had no controls. Doctors gave us prescriptions, and we got them from the pharmacy."

## From Cortisone to EPO

Cycling officials stuck for a way to ban a drug they could not detect got around EPO by counting red blood cells instead. However, an unusually high number didn't mean EPO was there, and so a rider couldn't be suspended or fined on a dope charge. Instead, he could be rested "for his health."

The limit for red cells, or haematocrit, was set at 50 percent. Dr. Beryl Greuet, of the Neuilly-Plaisance laboratory, calls it far too high. The population average is 42 percent, she says. Generous though the limit was, though, riders proved ungrateful enough to get round it. They bought pocket-sized centrifuges made in Germany, put a pinprick of blood into them and measured their haematocrit. There was enough time between the finish and the drug-test van to dose themselves with saline solution from an intravenous drip for 20 minutes to bring themselves back within legal limits.

The forerunner of EPO was cortisone and its variations. The argument was that the suprarenal gland couldn't produce enough hormones during a stage race or a hard season and needed help. Cortisone would delay exhaustion and speed up recovery. It would do it better than the steroids used in other sports, and it wouldn't build up bulk that would hold riders back in the mountains.

Tests showed that cortisone worked, but it also upset the balance between the hypophysis and the suprarenal gland; it also increased susceptibility to some illnesses and slowed or halted recovery from others. That was what was behind a confession in 1978 by the French rider Bernard Thévenet, winner of the Tour in 1975 and 1977.

"I have been doped with cortisone for three years," he said in an interview with *France-Vélo*, "and you see the result today; I can scarcely ride a bike."

Cortisone gave him two Tour wins. His third Tour saw him weeping on the first mountain, beaten like a novice. The year ended in a Paris hospital, where doctors diagnosed a list of troubles long enough to fill a medical dictionary.

The net is closing, though. Doctors from Lyon, Reims, and Strasbourg have all been disciplined, and several others were jailed in 1996 for complicity in doping. And it's closing on riders as well. The French amateur Yvan Cali was arrested in August 1996 while trying to present a forged prescription at Riom. Police who raided his house found growth hormone and EPO from four hospital pharmacies in the area. "I knew the hospitals well because I went there so often," Cali told the court. "That's how I got started with break-ins."

Cali was just a minnow, an unknown. Not so Gianni Bugno, world road champion in 1992. He landed a six-month suspended prison sentence and a fine of nearly $5,000 in December 2002 for buying and stocking amphetamine. In the dock with him at Kortrijk, Belgium, and similarly condemned and penalized were his father Giacomo, the soigneur Tiziano Morassut, and the former Belgian rider Edouard Vanhulst. The trial followed the 1999 De Panne three-day race in northern Belgium, when Bugno worked for the Italian Mapei team. The courier company DHL was about to deliver a parcel addressed to Mapei, when officials grew suspicious and called the police.

The parcel, with Bugno's name and address on the label, held amphetamines. The police moved in, surrounded Mapei's hotel, and stopped the race during its penultimate stage. It emerged that Morassut had sent the packet and that Vanhulst had supplied the drugs. Drugs by mail order. So much more convenient.

# 14. The Shadows Behind the Festina Affair

It seems like nobody truly cared about drug-taking in the days before Tom Simpson's death on Mont Ventoux. If that's what bike-racers needed to make a living, well, who was to blame them? If anything, people sympathized. Cycling was a hard sport easily appreciated by working-class men who spent all week in a factory, in fields, or down mines. They knew what hard muscular work was like. If bike-riders took something to stand the pace, who was to blame them?

Rik van Steenbergen, World Champion on the road in 1949, 1956, and 1957, and winner of 1,314 races on the track, justified events in the light of Simpson's death: "Sometimes I had to ride in Paris and then immediately after the race get into my car and drive for ten hours to Stuttgart, where I was back on my bike again. Things like that happened every day. There was nothing you could do.

"An organizer wanted this star and that star on his bill and he paid handsomely for it. Another organizer wanted those same stars a day later. The top riders were obliged to be fresh each time and they couldn't do that without stimulants. Nobody could or ever will be able to do that without stimulants because there are no such things as supermen. Doping is necessary in cycling."

Others, like Jean Bobet, were wise after the event. "I accuse professional cyclists of being so busy racing that they have no time to train," he said. "I reproach those in charge of cycle-racing teams for not having thrown out all the charlatans and soigneurs and replaced them by doctors and proper masseurs."

But did it make any difference? Have any of the deaths, ruined lives, and falsified results persuaded anybody of anything? Has it stopped old riders breaking into hospitals or running drugs rings, or shady outsiders distributing Eastern European drugs? Is there, since Simpson's day, a greater or a lesser application of drugs "of which nobody knows the secondary effects," as the former rider Alain Bondue put it, as he added with a smile: "Brigitte Bardot [film star become animal campaigner] should be happy; no more need for rats or guinea-pigs in laboratories — just use cyclists instead."

In most ways it has actually become worse. Compared to the medical treatment and human engineering that riders get within the rules today, the drugs that Simpson and his contemporaries took outside the rules were mild. Riders who have had their blood changed into something the body could never manage itself, and all within the rules, have had more done to them than Simpson ever did to himself. In many cases the drugs are not legal, or legal but illegitimately applied, and in some cases the drugs haven't even passed their testing stage or, worse, they have been tested and rejected. And still the boundaries are pushed.

No wonder governments took an interest. No wonder the police got involved. And no wonder the more their efforts were frustrated by the very victims they were setting out to save, the more determined they became. That's what makes 1998 the more dramatic, why many wonder just who was behind it, who knew what, and who tipped off whom. And why, according to lawyers of one of the men at the center, the whole business was a spat between two ideologies sharing the responsibilities in the government France.

The Festina raids weren't in themselves new. They were an updated version of Bordeaux and all those changing-room raids in Belgium. Nor did they end with Festina. They were repeated in the Giro d'Italia in 2001 — something which suggests that bike riders are committed dope-takers, too terrified to stop or too stupid to learn. The Festina story may no longer involve the team and its management, but it is far from finished. It has rumbled on ever since with trials of riders great and small all over France.

The story is that on 8 July 1998, Willy Voet was crossing from Belgium into France at the wheel of a new Fiat given to the Festina team for the Tour de France. Teams have their own cars, but it's a condition of the Tour that they use vehicles supplied by an event sponsor — Fiat in this case. Voet planned to catch the ferry from Calais to Dover, drive across England and then take the longer crossing to Ireland for the start of the Tour in Dublin.

The tickets were in his briefcase, the team's supplies were behind his seat, and his only worry was that he was tired after a short night's sleep. Only a small worry, though, solved by taking a *pot belge*.

Voet, the son of a train conductor who played semiprofessional soccer for Mechelen, had spent all his life in cycling. His family lived in a house bought from the money that soccer brought. The son, though, preferred cycling and joined Mechelen's club, the Dijlespurters, when he was 15. Among those he raced against as a junior were Eddy Merckx, Herman van Springel, and Walter Godefroot. The competition was stiff, Merckx in particular already winning 30 races a year.

Voet took his first drugs in a bike race when he was 18, in 1962. A friend called Gérard handed him two amphetamine pastilles, one to take 30 minutes before the start, the other halfway through the race. "Go on," he said. "You're going well and you'll be racing in front of your family." He wouldn't say where

Willy Voet, the Belgian *soigneur* who was caught red-handed in what has become known as the Festina Affair, wrote about his "30 years of trickery," as he called it, in professional cycling in his book *Massacre à la chaîne* (literally, "Chain Massacre," translated under the title *Breaking the Chain*).

he'd got them. It wasn't long before Voet knew all the likely sources. It became his job. Profession: doper of cyclists, a.k.a. soigneur.

Voet, a Dutch-speaking Belgian, moved to France to work with French professional teams, and learned excellent French, though with a tendency to address everyone with the informal and sometimes impertinent "*tu*" instead of the more formal "*vous*." He was at home as much in France as in Belgium, and it was no problem to go to Evry, near Paris, to collect the car and then go back to Belgium to visit the team's physician, a family doctor in Ghent called Erik Rijckaert.

Rijckaert and Voet loaded the new car with a treasure trove of dubious drugs, many of which were illegal in cycling. Some, with appealing bizarreness, Voet used to store behind the vegetables in his refrigerator. "It never bothered my wife," he said afterwards, "not because she had less space for her carrots but because she always assumed the drugs were innocent."

The stash, removed from its leafy surroundings, was placed in red and blue insulated bags behind the back seat. It included 234 doses of EPO, 160 capsules of testosterone and 60 doses of Asaflow, an aspirin-like drug to thin the blood for the same reason that Knud Enemark Jensen took Ronicol — because it helps the heart beat faster. There were also amphetamines and other drugs, including a personal dose of *pot belge* pushed down his underpants. Other than the *pot belge*, which riders wouldn't have used in the Tour, the other drugs were either undetectable in drug tests or allowed in limited quantities.

The drugs had been picked up in the car park of a Buffalo Grill (France's biggest restaurant chain) near Mérignac airport at Bordeaux. Voet, who had been banned from driving for repeated speeding, was driven there in an unmarked Peugeot 306 by his elder daughter, Carine. He made the trip each February and June. This time the weather was awful, the supplier was late and he and Carine — who knew nothing about the nature of the trip — went for a meal in the restaurant before returning to the car to wait behind moving windscreen wipers for the other car. When it arrived, the drivers maneuvered trunk to trunk and the cartons were loaded into Voet's car. It was worthy of a spy film.

Voet made his final call before the Tour at Rijckaert's house. The doctor wished him well and told him to be careful, and Voet waved and set off for home and, after that, for Calais. The obvious route across the border was the A14, the *autoroute* that forms part of the trans-European E17. It speeds through the middle of Roubaix and Lille, merged cities on the French border, and anybody who chose to drive through the congested city center instead would need to have a good reason.

Voet had a good reason. The borders of most of European Union countries and of Norway and Iceland have been open since March 1995, since the Schengen treaty signed in the Luxembourg city of that name. It completed the process of freedom of movement for people and goods across borders. Customs officials still existed, but they were rare and rarely paid any attention. There was a chance they'd be interested in a cycling team car, though, and Voet knew of the rich pickings in the Dutch TVM car some months earlier. So had Rijckaert, which is why he warned him to be careful.

Voet says he doesn't know "to this day" why he took a minor road so insignificant that his Michelin map didn't even give it a color. It runs from the Belgian village of Dronkaard toward Mont Halluin, in the French district of Neuville-en-Ferran. The detour added nearly an hour to the journey, but for Voet it was worth it. Whether he'd calculated it or not, it seemed unlikely there had be customs men there at 6:30 on a Tuesday morning. But there were: a mobile unit, a "routine check," as French border police insisted.

Voet came to a stop, worried he was as high as a kite. They ordered him to open the car. The stash could not have been easier to find. Did Voet have a prescription for it? You can picture them smirking as they asked the question. Voet said he didn't, that he was *"sans instruction préalable d'aucune nature,"* as the report put it afterwards: no prescription of any sort.

He was in trouble. Drugs and medicines are among rare exceptions to Europe's open borders. Individuals can cross with three months' supply of the normal dose. A prescription for more than three months would have seen Voet in the clear. Even without a prescription, he could have split the load with others and each would have cleared Customs with suspicion but no trouble. Voet was either naive or confident.

The border officials took him into their mobile cabin and told him to strip. If the unusual quantity of equally unusual drugs weren't enough to convince them they were on to something, the *pot belge* that fell out of his underpants was. Nobody on earth could justify to any nation's guardians of social integrity that he had a legitimate reason to have a cocktail of heroin, cocaine, amphetamine and lord knows what else shoved into his underwear.

Voet's journey to the Tour de France was over. So was his career. The police took him to Lille police station, where he was still so unsure of the situation that he kept saying he had a ferry to catch and that he had to get there in time. His world caved in when detectives found more drugs at the Festina warehouse. He confessed, now worried that he was about to become a scapegoat for what he saw was organized doping in the team and practices he was sure went on everywhere else as well.

More drugs were found in a car belonging to a French Big Mat team, backed by a building supplies warehouse chain. Riders from the TVM team, whose car had been searched earlier in the year, were arrested. A Spanish official was questioned, and the Spanish walked out of the Tour, just as they had decades earlier in the Tour of Britain.

By the first rest day, no fewer than 23 people had been arrested. The Festina team was disqualified en masse at 10:55 AM on July 17, a decision which had the organizer, Jean-Marie Leblanc, in tears.

Bruno Roussel, who ran the team, admitted that he had lost control of it to Rijckaert, whom he had met in 1992 and whom the riders respected more than Roussel for the drugs he could supply. The team, he said, had a dope fund to which riders contributed.

Voet, who was Erik Rijckaert's assistant, confessed: "Erik was one of the precursors of organized doping regimes within teams. For him there was no alternative: success meant using doping products. But he tried to channel it, to organize it so that riders didn't risk their health. He introduced them to doping to some extent, but with clarity of thought that cost him dearly."

The idea that he tried to limit the doping that he encouraged is legitimate. Riders referred to him jokingly as Dr. Punto, a Punto being the smallest car in the Fiat range. Fiats are made in Italy, and doses available there were much larger than what Rijckaert prescribed. Even so, team officials say that one result of attempts to keep doping under control was that some riders did deals with suppliers of their own, which spoiled both the purpose and the supervision.

So, how did the Festina affair happen? Just how did a customs unit come to be by the roadside at dawn on a summer morning in time to catch Willy Voet? Why just that road of the dozens that cross the border a few hundred meters apart. If Voet insists he doesn't know why he took that road, how would customs have known? Perhaps after all it was just a guess, that — as Voet said subsequently — the road turned out to be a favorite for small-time drug-carriers. Maybe we'll never know.

Customs aren't likely to say if they had a tip-off or if they were looking specifically for Voet. But Festina and Rijckaert were well known, Festina for earlier doping problems, and Rijckaert because he had been named as a supplier of EPO in a court case involving a Dutch rider. He had also been with the Dutch PDM team when it fell victim to an unexplained mass illness in the 1991 Tour, dropping out.

Hein Verbruggen, president of the UCI, said on July 17: "We already had our doubts about the team over the case of Christophe Moreau's positive test in June for anabolic steroids, which Roussel told me personally was the fault of a masseur. However, our inquiries suggested it was more than just the masseur who was involved, and in any case it is more the environment that the masseur works in than the person himself which must be questioned. Sadly our suspicions look to have been confirmed by what has happened."

The Tour teams were presented to fans in Dublin on Friday July 10, with news of Voet's arrest not yet confirmed but the center of discussion. That evening, there was a reception in the gardens of Phoenix Park, the official residence of the Irish president. Roussel was invited, mingled with the other French-speaking guests, and recognized France's elf-like sports minister, Marie-George Buffet. She gave him an immediate smile. A knowing smile.

"As I found out later," Roussel said, "she already knew all about the arrest, the analyses [of what had been found in Voet's car], and everything else."

Roussel — "not the first man to seek the headlines," as Erwann Menthéour puts it — found his personal distress growing ever deeper. A phone call from Voet's wife had confirmed that the team's soigneur was in jail; the police were moving in.

He engaged a Paris lawyer, Bertrand Lavelot. Lavelot was well-known for defending riders in doping trials and himself closely linked with Bernard Sainz, or Dr. Mabuse. He was legal adviser to the Française des Jeux team and came with the recommendation of Christophe Moreau, one of Roussel's riders.

It was Lavelot who recommended he add Thibault de Montbrial to the team. De Montbrial's law firm was used to affairs that attracted journalists, he said. That looked like being welcome experience. The next reason, though, puzzled him.

"You also need a specialist law firm with leanings to the Left," Lavelot insisted. The link hadn't yet formed in Roussel's mind between Voet's arrest and the smile he'd had from Buffet. He knew, of course, that Buffet, the communist sports minister in a broad-Left coalition under prime minister Lionel Jospin, had tightened up the Herzog anti-doping law and its successors. She had made drugs in sport and on the street a passion of the Jospin government. Roussel could hardly have been unaware of that, but he had to ask Lavelot what he meant.

"The whole thing stinks," Lavelot said enigmatically. "It's part of a political battle between the Left and Right." There was no further explanation.

"The phrase kept going round my head," Roussel recalled. "Lavelot had given me the first piece of the jigsaw, but it was only some months later that I could put the rest together."

His argument is that Festina's downfall began, not when Voet crossed the Belgian border but months earlier, in April. It was then that Agnès Pierret, the administrative director of the Société du Tour de France, had called to ask if the President's wife could watch the team test the time-trial course at Corrèze, southeast of Limoges.

The President's wife in France doesn't have the clout of her American counterpart, and most wives have been politically invisible. Bernardette Chirac, on the other hand, was outspoken and as well known as her husband Jacques. To understand the rest, you have to understand French politics. So, as briefly as I can, here's what you need to know:

Chirac is a longtime politician of the right. He was born in Paris in 1932 and educated at, among other places, Harvard. His first political success was at Ussel, near Corrèze, where he won a parliamentary seat in 1967. That's significant.

The running of France is divided between the Prime Minister, who runs internal affairs, and the President, who conducts broad policy at home and all French policy abroad. The President and the Prime Minister are elected at different times, so it's possible to have one from the left and one from the right. The two then bicker like fury, even in public, but make the best of it.

Chirac was a right-wing President Chirac was from the right and Prime Minister Lionel Jospin from the left. Chirac's election campaign in 1995 had had the support of the Amaury Sport organization, which not only organizes the Tour de France but also publishes newspapers, and from Richard

Virenque, France's most colorful rider. Events also showed that Chirac had the private support and even friendship of the Tour organizer, Jean-Marie Leblanc.

The election ended with none of France's many political parties having a majority, although there were more on the left than on the right. Lionel Jospin, the bespectacled, white-haired Prime Minister with the air of a professor, had to form a coalition with other parties besides his own Socialists to outgun Chirac. His payoff to the Communists, a moderate force in France, included giving the Ministry for Sports and Youth to Marie-George Buffet. There she was expected to have little influence and could be largely forgotten.

Buffet saw things differently and started work in a frenzy. News emerged that she had gone through the files left by her predecessor, when Chirac was Prime Minister, and, said a report in *Libération* on 20 December 2000, she had found a lot left undone. She immediately wrote her own doping laws and brought in tighter controls on the Tour de France.

That's the context. Now for Bernardette Chirac.

She and her husband were committed to living in the Presidential palace in Paris, where they addressed each other by the formal and old-fashioned *vous*. But she remained loyal to the Corrèze area, where her husband's career started, and she knew TV cameras would follow her if she followed France's favorite team testing the time-trial course. It would show the Chirac in a good light and bring publicity to a poor, sparsely populated, and under-industrialized area.

Roussel took the call from Agnès Pierret but explained as nicely as he could that it was to be a working day and that Bernardette Chirac and a phalanx of reporters would get in the way. Then, Roussel says, Jean-Marie Leblanc himself came on the line and begged him to agree, telling him that all France knew that this was Festina's big year, that a Festina rider could win, and that, with luck, it would be a Frenchman, Richard Virenque.

Roussel buckled under so much pressure and agreed. And so, on June 23, he drove behind his team with Bernardette Chirac in his passenger seat. He found her charming and lively, but noted with cynical amusement her political talent in pointing out every monument, every model farm, every grazing cow for the benefit of the cameras of the state-owned France 2 television station. Not forgetting, probably, to mention the scandalous lack of investment she considered Lionel Jospin had offered the area. She and Virenque were happy to pose for as long as the photographers wanted when the drive was over.

The film was to be aired on July 18, the day the Tour reached the area. It was never aired, and probably now lies on the shelves of INA, the French national film archive in Paris. July 18 was the day, in the back room of the Chez Gillou café in Corrèze, that Virenque begged Leblanc to keep his team in the Tour. And the day that Leblanc threw it out.

"He made a very moving plea to be allowed to stay in the Tour, but we've made the decision and we can't change it," Leblanc said.

According to testimony at the trial, Virenque then received a call from President Chirac, sympathizing, and asking him to accept the decision. Reports said, too, that Leblanc spent the night after the disqualifications with Jacques and Bernadette Chirac at the Bity chateau at Sarran.

Lavelot's argument didn't suggest anybody's personal involvement. But, he said, nabbing a soigneur and his drug-laden car and then disqualifying the team he was to have looked after was a superb chance for Marie-George Buffet to push through the changes she wanted. The more she could change — and the wish was heartfelt in both sport and on the streets — the more she would also expose what she saw as the laxity of the previous right-wing government.

The whole thing was balanced almost on an absurdity: The only offense, other than the *pot belge* shoved down his underwear, seemed to be that Voet had tried bringing controversial, but not in themselves illegal, drugs into France without a prescription. That is not the stuff on which politics turns. It could have made a decent headline in any customs' men's trade magazine but, frankly, it would have been pretty ho-hum even in Roubaix and Lille. It's not even obvious why the Festina team was disqualified anyway. It may have been implicated, even disgraced, but none of the riders had turned up positive in dope tests, and Voet's doping supplies had got no more than a few miles outside Belgium.

Festina was sacrificed for the reputation of the Tour, says Roussel, not for any crime. Better a city burns than an empire falls. Someone somewhere had contrived the whole business for personal ends. Yes, there was no denying that Festina had a drug fund, that its riders paid into it, that its doctor administered it, that there was shame in the household. But that had been going on there and elsewhere for years. It was just that now, for some deeper reason, it was the right time to blow the whole thing up.

Roussel says he had worked all this out by the time the post-Festina trial at Lille was coming to an end. By then, Richard Virenque had abandoned his foolish insistence that he was whiter than white and had muttered the words *"Oui, je me suis dopé"* ("Yes, I was doped"). His offense, without the hypocrisy and lying, was no greater than anyone else's. Had he owned up in the first place, the whole business could have ended sooner. If what someone wanted was the protracted agony of tearing off a plaster slowly rather than giving it a good rip, Virenque had unintentionally played into their hands.

Roussel went for dinner one night, he said, with one of the policemen most closely involved in the case. By then they had got to know each other quite well. There was no personal antagonism, because in France the investigation is carried out not by the police but by a judge. Was it right to think,

Virenque on the Tour de France victory podium for the Polka-Dot jersey in 1999. He vehemently denied that he had taken any drugs, and insisted he should not be punished along with the others involved in the Festina Affair (he rode for Festina at the time). Subsequently he was caught anyway and sheepishly announced, *"Oui, je me suis dopé"* ("Yes, I was doped")

Roussel asked, that Willy Voet had been *balancé* [loosely: thrown to the lions] by someone within cycling?

"You'll understand that I can't really tell you," the policeman replied.

Roussel said that he then mentioned a single name — whose name that was he has not revealed. The policeman answered: "Sorry, I can't confirm that," but with a knowing smile. And, of course, without denying it. He couldn't confirm it but he hadn't denied it either.

That, Roussel says, convinced him his guess had been right. The whole thing, he said, was a setup from inside cycling. The most frustrating bit of the story is that it ends there, that we're missing the name. Cynics would say that it was in Roussel's interests to concoct a conspiracy theory, that it would shift the blame or at least divert the pressure from him. And that would be true, es-

## Whatever Happened to… the Festina Four?

Roussel left cycling to work for a building company after the Festina trial, in which he prides himself on being the only official to take full responsibility for what happened. He no longer has any official role in cycling.

Willy Voet stayed in France and spent years of unemployment after 1998, despite 30 years in top-level cycling. "For 30 years, the word 'doping' never passed my lips: even today it's difficult for me to say 'so-and-so was doped,'" he says. He was ruled *persona non grata* by the Tour de France and shunned elsewhere. He is still without a job.

Erik Rijckaert never recovered from three months in jail and died on 26 January 2001. He was buried in his home town of Zotergem, Belgium, on 3 February 2001. His friends and some of the patients at his everyday practice were at the funeral, but Voet and Richard Virenque were among the few from the cycling world.

Marie-George Buffet, born May 7 1949 at Sceaux, southern Paris, was French sports minister from 4 June 1997 to 5 May 2002. She lost her job in the 2002 elections, when the country swung to the (moderate) right, behind Jacques Chirac, rather than accept Jean-Marie Le Pen, his extreme-right opponent. Her laws remain on the statute book and she remains in politics.

pecially if it had happened in the heat of the inquiry. But he didn't make the claims until 2001, by which time he had left the sport. He works now not against the Ministry for Sports and Youth but with it, visiting towns in western France, where he lives, to talk to young riders, club officials and coaches, persuading them of the dangers and futility of drug-taking, taking with him riders such as Xavier Jan, Stéphane Heulot, and Marc Gomez.

"In a sense, the circle has been completed," he says. "I have gone back to my original motivation, the one that made me an educator [his former job]."

Sadly, there are still many who have to learn. It seems the Festina affair did little within the professional peloton, especially outside France. The only real difference with the drug raids on the Giro in 2001 was the quality of the setting. Instead of a back road near the unlovely city of Roubaix, it was the Hotel Astoria, one of the best hotels in San Remo. It stands in the Corso Matuzia, 600 meters from the sea and about the same distance from the city's casino. Normally it's full of affluent tourists and businessmen — anonymous people with suits, briefcases, and cell phones.

It's the kind of place where the organizers of the Giro d'Italia like to put riders because it gives a good impression of the race. Unfortunately, events in 2001 took an unpredictable turn. Or an unwelcome one, anyway.

"We were about to go into the restaurant for dinner, when we saw people near the rooms," said Max Sciandri, known in Italy as Italian but identified by his racing license as British. "We were told we couldn't move. They started searching the rooms, the suitcases, backpacks, everything."

Operation Four Leaf Clover had begun. It was bigger and better than the Festina raids of 1998. The national drugs squad, the NAS, had been sent by Luigi Bocciolini, the Florence prosecutor, after more than a week of following riders, listening to calls, examining a hotel, and going through trash. They met customs police dispatched by Paola Cameran, who was following an investigation into one particular team and an incident in which a rider's parents had been found with a camper van loaded with drugs. Cameran is a magistrate in Padua; in Italy as in France, magistrates conduct inquiries as well as handle the trial.

The raid lasted little more than 15 minutes, but riders were questioned until 1 AM. Rooms were ransacked, vehicles pulled apart. There were reports of a rider jumping from a window to avoid detection, of plastic bags dropped from the upper stories of the hotel, of a masseur crawling on his knees through the garden to hide a bag behind bushes. The press reported of drugs thrown into the Mediterranean and fished out by police launches.

There were so many medications found that police carried them away in 10-liter paint buckets. They filled a small truck. Some were harmless and legal. But there were also little-known blood-enhancers such as HemAssist and RGR-13, undetectable replacements for EPO, the drug for which two riders had already been thrown out of the Giro. Some of the other drugs hadn't progressed beyond clinical trials and at least one had been withdrawn in Europe by its manufacturer.

The police took 250 sworn statements and placed 50 riders and as many masseurs, managers, and team doctors under inquiry. The names included some of the biggest in the race. Riders went on strike and the day's stage was canceled. Later they met in a wood-paneled room at the Astoria and said they'd continue the Giro "with the aim of saving the values of cycling."

Cynics heard the statement with a smile. Their lack of confidence was justified two days later when the second best rider was pulled out by his team after admitting that what the police had found in his room were indeed drugs. At that stage the analyses hadn't been completed yet.

Dario Frigo, a man with quaffed blond hair, came up with the entertaining justification that, yes, they had been drugs but, no, he hadn't intended to use them. A week later, Italy canceled all races for six days, "to make a sport without shadow," according to the president of the Italian Cycling Federation, Giancarlo Ceruti. In practice it was a week of mourning and shame. The row, the inquiries, the court cases, and the ever-expanding web of inquiries and implications were still going on years later. Just like the Festina affair.

# 15. May the Best Man Win...

A nd now, how about learning of some ways to win a race unconventionally, and some ideas on how to lose one equally unconventionally. Indeed,
it seems neither winning nor losing is always quite what it seems — and as
those who believe in the sport feel it should be.

Years back, the end of the 1970s, I took a team of friends to race in Holland. I had just started becoming fascinated by the place; it seemed to me that
everything in Holland in general and Dutch cycling in particular was perfect.

We went to a town called Roosendaal, in the cycling heartland of Brabant
province, and stayed with friends from the club after they had been our guests.
I was impressed by the club jerseys, which were white with a scarlet diamond
to mimic the Faema colors of Eddy Merckx, and the way that even no-hopers
would say before each race that they were feeling good and this could be their
big day. It seemed a long way from the faintly self-defeating attitude of British
riders.

Our best rider emerged as a tall lad with a slightly sunken chest, called
Jeremy Patterson. He had just moved to our little club from the bigger one
further down the valley, and to see him doing well in Dutch criteriums in our
colors rather than theirs was a special pleasure.

Dutch criteriums are run on a circuit in the center of a village or town,
with the entire area closed off and spectators charged to watch. The proceeds
from the entry fee are split with the local council that provides the barriers.
The occasion is completed by loudspeakers all around the kilometer-long
course, powered by an announcer who talks and talks until he can think of

nothing else to say — and sometimes beyond that point — and then plays a record while he sinks another bottle of Heineken.

The commentators are always desperate for new things to talk about and so halfway through our third race I was called to the flatbed truck which was his temporary podium.

"Are your races in England like this?" he asked.

I said they weren't, that England was hillier — everywhere is hillier than most of Holland — and races were over 20 km rather than 1 km circuits, on roads that weren't closed to traffic, for prizes that rarely went beyond the first five and certainly not to the first 30 that Dutch races offered. And I said that you thought you'd laid on a real public spectacle if you got more than a huddle of mothers and friends at the finish.

I don't think he was really listening and I imagine the crowd didn't really understand. I was doing my best in Dutch but I doubt it was impressive. Then he asked a question so astonishing that I had to ask him to repeat it in English.

"Will your boy Jeremy win today?" he asked. I don't want to belittle Jez but the idea had never occurred to me. He was doing well and in a break of a dozen, but he admitted himself that he was there to learn, not to start forest fires. I explained that as best I could in the moments after the break had passed.

The riders could hear it as they went round the circuit, thanks to the loudspeakers, but in the effort of riding at what seemed like 50 km/h, they probably heard only "Jeremy" and "win" and none of my answer. So I thought Jeremy the unknown Englishman would win, did I? Best they did something about that, then...

On the next lap they maneuvered my talented but naive friend to the inside of the road, then refused to swing over as they approached a shallow chicane of a protruding sidewalk. There was a grating noise, a grinding of metal on concrete and stone, and the gasp of the crowd. Jeremy in his mauve jersey with white trim was flattened on the roadside with attendants in the green and white of the Dutch first-aid organization running to help him.

The crowd sympathized, the commentator sympathized. But it was just an Englishman and he wasn't used to this style of racing. Had his "manager" not just said so?

Like Jeremy, I returned to the area to live soon afterwards, Jeremy as a bike rider, I as a journalist. By then, Jez was making a name, had won friends and a small reputation. There was now no way he'd be put into the sidewalk. Sheepishly, one of the guys concerned came over to apologize.

"We didn't know him then," he said. "We didn't want to be beaten by an outsider."

He wasn't the first, nor the last. Outside Ghent, at Wachtebeke, lives a messianic-looking man with a long mournful face and beard who's spent much of the last few decades working, in his own words, as "one of the best-paid crane-drivers in Belgium." His name is Graham Webb, his gloomy look is misleading, and he was world amateur road race champion in 1967.

He won that race alone and stood on the podium in a rain-soaked rainbow jersey so small on his giant body that it only just reached his shorts. He too raced in Holland, not far from Roosendaal, immediately before the championship. The story he told me in the front room of his house in Canary Lane (although in Dutch, of course) is one of the best:

> My first race was in Breda, in really awful weather. It was on cobbled roads and they were using a dirt track on the side of the road with holes you could put a whole wheel in, and they were covered with water. It was really thrilling because I had something I could dig my teeth into. I was pushing and shoving all the time [Webb is 6ft 4in tall] and I'd get to the back of the echelon, riding on the grass, on the road, on the cobbles, on the road — up the dykes and down them, and I was really enjoying myself.
>
> And there was this one chap and he was really dangerous, and he kept pushing me, and I got to the back of the echelon and he was trying not to come to the front. And he was shouting "*Pas op! Pas op!*" [watch it, buddy] all the time. I don't know if it was very sporting of me or not, but I put him in the ditch, not really to get rid of him, but I wanted the other riders to know I wasn't going to play around. It was only a grass ditch and I knew he wasn't going to hurt himself, and after that I didn't have to push any more.
>
> At one stage we went up this dyke. The blokes in front started to slip on the wet cobbles and mud, and I was having to take corners wider and wider, and I slipped into the grass and over the dyke and into the sea [river] — seven meters. I was covered in black mud. I dragged my bike out of the water and up the bank, and I got back on and started chasing. I caught a few who'd got shot off and finished 16th, covered in slime and freezing cold, in my first race.

Anyway, I was more or less famous from my first race in Holland. I was a hero, and I didn't know why. A hero for being 16th. I couldn't understand it.

The next race was on a course more like Jeremy's, a kilometer round with half a dozen corners and a road surface of *klinkers*, the herringbone-pattern-placed bricks that visiting bike riders assume are cobbles — until they get to ride cobbles. There were primes, intermediate prizes, every few laps. Webb, who didn't speak Dutch at the time, and couldn't understand the announcements, and anyway had more history as a track rider than a roadman, joined in the sprints because he didn't know what was going on. He soon learned there was money on offer.

> We came round for the prime and I took it and I was piling the pressure on in the corners and I was left with one chap on my wheel. There were no real long stretches to burn him off, so I thought I'd have to get rid of him. I went into the chicane. I thought if he tries to follow me he'll crash into a wall. I had this feeling I could corner better than anyone.
>
> Sure enough he wrapped himself round a lamppost trying to follow me, which was very courageous of him, trying to the death to follow me. I've got a lot of respect for that. Anyway, I was away. I could have lapped them but I wasn't sure whether I'd have to sprint again for the primes. So I just left them hanging there. I won 98 primes plus the *klassement* [an overall competition for prime winners]. I'd won enough money to pay for six months' bed and board.

There aren't, and weren't, many riders with so much talent, and it's no surprise in retrospect — although it *was* to those at home who remembered him only as a gangling pursuit rider with a miserable face — that he became World Champion. There are plenty of riders with the muscles, weight, and daring to throw themselves about in races, but what makes Webb so different is that he speaks of it not only with innocence but with respect for those he beat.

The best man won when Webb became World Champion, in 1967. The race came together with 32km to go and Webb, who'd been training 200–300 km a day, took 30 meters from a corner.

"There was another corner and 700 meters to go, and I thought if I can take the last corner without falling on my head, I was world champ."

He was, but his first thought as he raised his arm wasn't to rejoice but to wonder whether he had miscounted those ahead of him. Four riders had also tried their luck. Were some still in front? Had he passed them all? The intense look on his face as he crossed the line wasn't exhaustion but terror that he might be celebrating a championship he hadn't won.

He would have looked daft if he had whooped with joy and then found he'd come fifth — although it *has* happened — but how likely is it that a rider sure of victory would rather not win at all? In 1977, the German rider Didi Thurau, an angelic figure with blond hair and bronzed skin, was leading the World Championship at San Cristobal, Venezuela, with the equally handsome Francesco Moser of Italy. The pair were a maiden's dream, and one of the two *had* to be World Champion.

Moser punctured seven kilometers from the line, and Thurau had only to attack for his rival, even with his talents as a world-class pursuiter and Hour record candidate, never to get back. Instead, he dithered and an astonished Moser caught up with him and beat him easily in the sprint.

"*C'est bizarre*," was how Jacques Anquetil put it, especially because he'd missed so many World Championships himself. Equally puzzled was Thurau's manager in the Raleigh team, the Dutchman Peter Post. "I've only ever known Thurau as someone who wanted to win," he said.

Rumors were rife. Moser wore the rainbow jersey and Thurau pulled off his red, yellow, and black Raleigh jersey at the end of the season and instead adopted the yellowish orange of his new IJsboerke team sponsored by a Belgian frozen-foods company.

Eventually it emerged that Thurau had not, as the rumors insisted, sold the victory to Moser. Instead, Staf Janssens, the head of IJsboerke, had let Thurau know that he didn't want him to spend his first year in the team in a rainbow jersey. His advertising would stand out more on a team jersey than if it was overpowered by rainbow bands. Thurau was a golden child, and any sponsor would want his return from such an expensive acquisition. Sadly, he turned out both costly and disappointing because his career fizzled out as quickly as it had started.

There are bike riders all round the world who dream of nothing else but winning the Tour or becoming champion of the world. The *maillot arc-en-ciel* was regarded with an almost religious respect for many years and advertising was never added to it. A sponsor would do without, content that his man was subtly but convincingly associated with the firm that paid his wages. The world road champion was sometimes not even asked to wear a number, the jersey being considered such an identifiable trophy.

Things changed with the rise of television and the decline of bicycle makers as sponsors. Riders and team managers began hunting for sponsors outside the industry. The first *extra-sportif* of the modern era (there had been outside sponsors in the early days of the sport) was a soccer betting company called ITP in Britain in 1947. There were others in Spain as well, but both countries were too far from big-time cycling for officials to worry about a breach of rules that insisted that teams represent bike companies.

Then a balding Italian called Fiorenzo Magni negotiated a deal with the makers of Nivea face cream in 1954 — a humorous episode because Magni was not the kind of man to be associated with face cream. He was followed at the start of the 1960s by the Frenchman Raphaël Géminiani, who signed the St.-Raphaël aperitif company that shared his name. The coup worked both ways. The team rode Géminiani's own bikes, or bikes made under his name, and having St.-Raphaël on the shirts emphasized that link while bringing in outside money.

The St.-Raphaël deal upset the Tour de France, where bosses realized that advertisers who once put their money into the Tour's sister newspaper, *L'Équipe*, could put it into team sponsorship instead. The Tour is nothing if not a commercial operation.

The race exerted enormous influence over both French and world cycling. Before long the rumpus embroiled the UCI. Angry officials told Géminiani to call off the deal, that it was illegal, that it turned cyclists into nothing more than sandwich-board men. Géminiani wasn't the kind of man to back down, though, and the stalemate lasted until Milan–San Remo, the first classic. But much can be achieved in cycling by ignoring the rules, cheating, and sometimes by lying.

Achille Joinard, the president of the UCI, said no with his lips but nodded yes with his head. Keen on tripping up the bumptious people at the Tour, and recognizing that cycling needed outside money, he forbade Géminiani from starting Milan–San Remo — but made sure the telegram arrived in Milan moments *after* the start.

That opened the way and firms from outside cycling saved the sport. Riders learned to shrug and accept the indignity of advertising washing machines, lemonade or anything else. And those sponsors, detached from tradition, saw no reason why their names shouldn't get as much exposure as possible. Especially in a country with a growing audience for cycling but, as yet, no television advertising.

Since then, the rainbow jersey and the *maillot jaune* have become so cluttered with advertising that they no longer stand out. Nobody is heard in a land where everybody shouts. The consequence is that sponsors value a champion in their ranks less and less. Bruno Roussel confirms this. He says: "To take part in the national championships was one thing, but to win it was another. Miguel Rodriguez, our boss, didn't look kindly on the idea that one of his own should hide his Festina jersey under the colors of the French flag, however prestigious they might be. 'I don't want to have anything to do with a national jersey,' he never stopped saying.

"He took his argument as the team's investor still further. So, when I brought up the World Championship and its symbolic rainbow jersey, he was no more enthusiastic. 'I pay the riders all through the year to carry the name of my business,' he said, 'not to dress up like a paint factory.'"

If it doesn't matter to every sponsor, neither does a rainbow jersey concern some riders. They find it commercially more useful to help their rivals. Nobody suggests that a national team in the soccer World Cup could fall apart because players are from rival clubs. A goalkeeper doesn't let the ball through his hands because the man who's kicked it, even though from a different country, normally plays with him on the same team. And yet that's just what happens in cycling.

Those who refuse to be bound by national interest, or who come from countries too small to put up worthwhile teams, see no reason not to sell their services to anybody willing to pay. And sometimes for nothing if there's a team contract in the offing. The World Championship should be seen in that light: a straight race with subplots which confuse the story.

Shay Elliott of Ireland, for instance, threw away a World Championship in Salo in 1962 in favor of his French brother-in-law, Jean Stablinski. The Irishman had been away by himself when Stablinski and the Belgian Jos Hoevenaars caught him. Elliott made no attempt to chase when Stablinski attacked, however. It was pointless Hoevenaars chasing because Elliott would merely ride behind him and beat him in the sprint. The outcome: Stablinski became World Champion because Elliott let him. Stablinski returned the favor in the 1963 Tour when he slowed a break so Elliott could get back after a puncture, then let him attack with six kilometers to go so that he'd win at Roubaix and become the first English-speaker to wear the yellow jersey.

Elliott was talented, but he soon learned that there was more money in help-ing others win races than in winning himself. Even the best win only a few of the races they ride, so there are always those who'll pay to have their chances in-creased. Elliott admitted openly that he had regularly sold races to rivals.

The most notable example for which there is evidence was the 445 km London–Holyhead race in 1965. It was the longest unpaced event in the world, only Bordeaux–Paris being further. It was of little importance to any-one outside Britain, where the race linked the capital with a Welsh island, but it was important to the domestic semi-professionals who took part, as well as an opportunity for English-speaking professionals from the Continent to show their superiority. Their clan leader was Tom Simpson.

The race was a monster to organize under British conditions. Not only were the roads not closed off, but riders were expected to stop at traffic lights.

"I was in a small break with a few others, not far ahead of the field," Simpson remembered, "and we were approaching a set of traffic lights, some-thing I have never had to think about in a bike race for years. They were at red and Bill Bradley [a semi-professional] said 'Don't go! Stay here, Tom, or he'll get you.' When we moved off on the green, I saw what Bradley had meant: About 20 yards beyond the lights, hidden from us by a telephone box, was a police motorcyclist. He even had the cheek to grin at us when we rode by."

You'd think such a race would hardly be worthwhile for one of the best riders in the world, still less that he could persuade others to come from the continent with him. But Simpson knew the appeal of the race in Britain, and the importance it held in possibly persuading a British company to run a team with him as its leader. That would solve his employment problems, and so London–Holyhead, trivial or not, was a good race to win.

Simpson remembered: "Eventually we got a good break going, eight of us together for the last 50 miles or so. I won the sprint from Elliott with the Brit-ish champion, Albert Hitchen, getting third place."

What he doesn't say is that between the continentals' arrival and the finish at Holyhead, money had been promised if other riders let Simpson win, and more if they would help him do it. Elliott, as usual, was open to offers. If you look at photographs, it doesn't take much to see that he has his fingers on the brakes even before reaching the line.

Years later, another British continental, Vin Denson, confirmed what many suspected but *Cycling* had dismissed: that there had been a fix. Simpson was the best rider and the race — especially in 10 hrs. 49 min. for 275 miles, including a 5 AM start, traffic lights, roundabouts, unclosed roads, and fans carving up the bunch in their cars — wasn't exactly an everyday criterium. To that extent, it surprised no one that he won.

But, as Denson says: "We'd come to an arrangement that Tom would win because that's what people in England would want to see, and we gathered around him at the finish to protect him. The trouble was that Hitchen wasn't in on the deal and started coming through really fast. What you see in the picture is Elliott putting his brakes on, not so much to avoid beating Tom but to stop Hitchen coming through."

Arrangements like this weren't unusual. Benoni Beheyt, who had so much trouble with Rik van Looy in the World Championship in 1963, won Ghent–Wevelgem in that same year. He sprinted up the right side of the road and held another Belgian, Michael van Aerde, against the crowd. All quite legitimate and exciting. What is more curious is that in the middle of the road was Simpson in his long-sleeved Peugeot shirt. The gap between him, Beheyt, and Van Aerde is hard to assess looking back down the road, but it's clear he has as good a chance of winning as anyone else. Which makes it the odder that, despite his theatrical, openmouthed, elbows-out sprinting, he has his fingers on both brakes five meters before the line. You have to ask why.

Similarly, in 1961, Simpson won the Tour of Flanders in a sprint with Nino Defillipis of Italy. The situation was confusing because the finish banner had blown down and the finish line was indicated instead by a man with a red flag. Even so, the race had gone through the finish three times, and Simpson and Defillipis had been alone, so neither man's view of the line had been obstructed. The two sprinted and Simpson won.

"There was pandemonium," Simpson recalled. "He just could not believe he had been beaten, especially by me, since I had not at that time been regarded as a great sprinter. Immediately he lodged a protest that he did not see the line properly — that there was no finish banner marking it [but] there was no doubt he knew where it was."

For whatever reason, though, Defillipis had his fingers on his brakes before the line. It could be chance, it could be confusion, but the fact remains that they were there.

Simpson said: "The next thing I knew was that the Italians came to see me and asked me if I would agree to an "equal first" decision. Not on your life! They told me that an Italian had not won a classic since 1953, but I replied that an Englishman had not won one since 1896. I was not to be talked into or out of anything (…) Generally the hue and cry subsided, but it was weeks before the papers and the people stopped writing and talking about it."

That sort of thing made rumors inevitable when Simpson improbably outsprinted the giant German Rudi Altig to win the World Championship in Spain in 1965. Simpson, however, says the two just agreed to a straight sprint and that Altig doubtless believed he was the stronger — which he was — and considered it a good deal. There's no suggestion of anything underhand, only that such is the suspicion that surrounds professional racing that many find it hard to consider any unlikely outcome to be fair. As Elliott showed, trades in World Championships weren't unusual.

Michel Stolker told the Dutch publication *Wielerrevue* that in the 1961 World Championships in Berne, he had lost too many Dutch team-mates to hope for victory. That left him open to offers:

> Van Looy came up to talk to me. He said he'd seen how well I was riding. But [when a rider drops a hint like that] it puts you in a difficult position. So I had to go and talk to Jacques Anquetil [who wasn't Dutch either but was Stolker's boss the rest of the year] and find out whether he was going to try to win. If he'd said yes, I couldn't have ridden for Van Looy and I'd have had to have ridden for Anquetil instead.

Such is the complexity of the World Championship: a rider engaged to ride and win for Holland is approached by a Belgian but has to check with a Frenchman.

The World Championship at Zurich in 1946 looked like a certain victory for another tough Belgian, Marcel Kint. The so-called Black Eagle, because of his nose and the old-style black Belgian jerseys he wore, was born in 1914 and died only in March 2002, aged 87. He will probably always be cycling's longest-serving World Champion, having won the title ahead of Paul Egli of Switzerland at Valkenburg in 1938 and been unchallenged until 1946 because of the war.

A romantic story would have been completed if Kint could win again, at 32 and after an eight-year gap. He certainly wanted to. Like Rik van Looy, he promised to pay his teammates if he won, and sure enough, in the last kilometers he looked set to pay out the 15,000 francs. To everyone's surprise, though — not least Kint's — out of the bunch came another Belgian, Rik van Steenbergen. On his wheel was the Swiss rider Hans Knecht in his red jersey with a white cross. The two caught Kint who, unable to resist after riding so long by himself, saw Knecht ride by him for the rainbow jersey he thought would be his own.

The assumption was that van Steenbergen, who was known for his fondness for money, had engaged that fondness to get Knecht to the front. The row grew and developed into a national uproar. Years later, I went to see Van Steenbergen in his Spanish-style villa outside Antwerp. He was intrigued as to how I had obtained his unlisted phone number — puzzled rather than angry — but satisfied when I gave him the name of a journalist on *Het Volk*, the down-market Belgian daily for which I used to write.

Van Steenbergen warned me to watch out for his dog, which was nowhere as fierce as it seemed, he said, and persuaded his English wife to serve coffee while we sat in his main room. He was a cuddly, grey-haired avuncular character. This surely wasn't the man who had once insisted that the organizer at London's Herne Hill track empty the turnstiles, and even his own wallet, before he'd ride, still less a man who'd sell a World Championship. He looked so

## Whatever Happened to... Marcel Kint?

Kint was one of those epic pre-war Flemish roadmen to whom guts and courage mattered more than grace and elegance. Legend says he used to train on salted fish to get used to the thirst he'd feel in the Tour de France.

He rode as a pro from 1935 until 1951, rode the Tour five times — finishing ninth in 1936 and 1938 and winning six stages — and won Paris–Roubaix in 1943 and Flèche Wallonne in 1943, 1944, and 1945.

A crash in the 1947 six-day in Paris cracked his skull and he didn't race until 1949, when he won Ghent–Wevelgem. The post-championship rift with van Steenbergen didn't last: the two became regular partners in six-day events.

very different from the days when his hardness on a bike caused ripples of fear through the bunch.

He dismissed the championship as "bad luck," explaining, "Just as ever, there was no agreement between the Belgian riders whom they were going to ride for. Since nothing had been settled, I thought "Right, I'll take my chance." On the last lap, Marcel Kint attacked, the best rider in the world in those days, and took 25 seconds.

"Then I went, and on my wheel I had the Swiss, Knecht. I couldn't get him off. I had to pull out everything to get up to Kint. I swung over for the other guy, but he wouldn't come through. One kilometer from the line, I finally got up to Kint. At that moment, the guy on my wheel jumped away. I couldn't react, nor would Kint. We were beaten, the two best riders in the world."

Belgian fans weren't convinced it was so simple and demanded to know why Van Steenbergen had chased Kint in the first place, still less when he had a rider on his wheel. It would have been wonderful had Belgian riders taken both the gold and the silver, but van Steenbergen had either sold the race to Knecht or he had been guilty of the most astounding stupidity.

Rik van Steenbergen, shown here after one of his Paris– Roubaix victories, was one of Belgium's toughest riders. He was accused of (and vehemently denied) "selling" the 1946 World Championship to the Swiss rider Hans Knecht — against his countryman Rik Van Looy.

"The row got so bad that my manager, Jean van Buggenhout, said, 'Stay away for 14 days, stay out of Belgium.' It was a great scandal. Never in 22 years have I sold a World Championship. Then there was pressure on the Belgian federation that van Steenbergen shouldn't be picked any more."

He had to ride the 1949 Tour de France, a race for which he wasn't suited and never looked forward to, to get back his place in the World Championship team.

"I did it just to win a stage. I won the last one, 300 km to Paris, in the Parc des Princes. That was the breakthrough. It was settled, and I was back in the team."

Van Steenbergen, the showman, had calculated that he would never win one of the mountain stages because of his build. So, if it was going to be one of the other stages, Paris would be the one that everybody would notice. Even more so because it was the first finish in Paris to be televised live. And if winning on television got him into the World's team, so much the better because a rainbow jersey had commercial value to a track rider.

## Whatever Happened to… Shay Elliott?

Elliott's career dwindled with the decline in his strength and ability to work for others. Many who had gained from his services, official and unofficial, overlooked him when it came to giving help when he needed it. He lost money in a hotel venture at Locturdy in Brittany and his marriage to Jean Stablinski's sister, Marguerite, faltered, and she eventually left him. Elliott tried to make ends meet by writing a tell-all article about bribery and drug-taking for the London *Sunday People* and, mild though it was, it completed his exclusion from Continental racing.

He returned to Ireland and set up a metalworking business and raced briefly as a semi-professional in Britain. His father died in April 1971 and Elliott was found dead in his garage on May 4 the same year with a shotgun beside him.

In 1998, the year the Tour started in Dublin, Jean-Marie Leblanc laid a wreath on Elliott's grave in the churchyard at Kilmacanogue in County Wicklow.

There were echoes of the Kint-Van Steenbergen finish in the World Championship of 1982, at Goodwood in southern England. Two Americans were in the leading group as it approached the final hill. Out of it came one of them, Jonathon Boyer, sometimes known as Jacques or Jock, the first American to ride the Tour de France. He wasn't the immediate choice for a rainbow

## Whatever Happened to... Graham Webb?

Only three British riders have won the men's world road race championship. Tom Simpson is the single winner in the pro event, in 1965. The amateurs are Dave Marsh in 1922 (the year in which Britain organized the championships, filled the first three places... and had the promotion confiscated halfway because of poor organization and bad weather)... and Graham Webb in 1967.

As a boy, Webb used to ride from his home in Birmingham to the western city of Gloucester just to see if he could do it. Several times he collapsed in a ditch, literally, with exhaustion, but tried again week after week until he could do it.

On an everyday bike with steel rims and heavy tires, he rode his first 25-mile time-trial in 1:1:31, despite not knowing what was required of him, knocking his pump off and pulling a jammed chain from between the freewheel and chainstay — undoing the wheel nuts, and remembering to clean his hands on a cloth afterwards.

His pro career never happened, though. His toe-straps stretched into uselessness in Het Volk, his knee hurt unbearably in Kuurne–Brussels–Kuurne, and he says despairing team-mates abandoned him in Paris–Nice, so that he had to leave his bike in a pub and hitch a lift to his hotel from a spectator.

Things got worse, his knee deteriorated, and by the end of the year he was a forgotten hero. He joined a small team in Belgium and made a living, but it all ended as quickly as it started. He stayed in Belgium and won an unofficial Belgian national championship as a veteran. He still trains on the Ghent track and, retired now as a crane driver, spends his time in Belgium and neighboring Luxembourg.

He is largely forgotten in Britain.

jersey but wisely he gambled on surprise, knowing he would beat neither Beppe Saronni of Italy or Sean Kelly of Ireland if he stayed with them. And he hoped that the other American, the younger Greg LeMond, would keep things in order when a chase started.

LeMond was also no favorite, so Saronni and Kelly were more occupied with each other. Neither could afford to chase and blunt his chances of beating the other, but neither was there any point in leaving the race to a little-known American who had never won a big race.

The two were just working out their puzzle when LeMond solved it for them. Far from protecting Boyer, he set off in pursuit. Look at pictures and you can see Saronni looking at him with a smile. He was astonished, yes, but above all he was grateful. There was now no doubt Boyer would be caught, and there was no risk that Kelly would reach the finish any fresher than Saronni.

Boyer topped the hill and set his eyes on the finish. And then, as he clung to his dreams, thrashing past him came Kelly and Saronni and, showing no inclination to slow things down, his fellow countryman LeMond. Up behind came everyone else, and Boyer — perhaps thanks to LeMond but perhaps inevitably anyway — was left to come in 10th.

LeMond didn't win either. The victory went to Saronni. Had LeMond won, then Boyer would grudgingly have had to accept that at least there was an American in a rainbow jersey. As it was, it was clear that he felt that he had been stabbed in the back, and his demeanor showed that perfectly. LeMond, on the other hand, couldn't care less and even seemed surprised when reporters asked him why he'd done it.

"Because I wasn't part of a team," he said. "I paid for myself to come here. I had no help from the American Cycling Association. I covered all my own expenses, made all my own arrangements. There was no team in the meaning of a team. I rode for myself, I saw my chance and I took it."

LeMond is not the only rider who has declined to help someone from his own country. Freddy Maertens never hid his feelings for his Belgian rival, Eddy Merckx. The two could each win more than 50 races in a year, but while Maertens won many of his in Belgium, they were often just criteriums; Merckx had his greatest glories abroad but in real races. Maertens never won the Tour de France but Merckx won five.

Winning so much, however, made Merckx enemies. His rivals were also professionals, men who had to feed and house their families, and having Merckx snatch money away from them day after day did nothing to make their lives simpler. Not only that, but the more Merckx won and the more he rode for teams sponsored by foreign companies such as Molteni and Faema, the more he depressed wages at home. So many good riders went with Merckx as his domestiques that again the market in Belgium was deflated.

Maertens, who rode only for Belgian teams at the height of his career, objected to Merckx more than most. Their rivalry — felt, I suspect, by the flamboyant Maertens more than the established and less excitable Merckx — flared in the 1973 World Championship near Barcelona.

Maertens says he and others in the Belgian team were training on the course the previous afternoon when Tullio Campagnolo, the wealthy boss of the components firm, had driven alongside and warned: "At all costs Shimano must not win on Sunday." Campagnolo had monopolized the high-quality components market and most of the professional teams since the early 1950s. Shimano, however, had just started stealing some of its ground and it backed Maertens' trade team, Flandria. Maertens said he didn't know what to make of the alleged remark but says it became clear afterwards.

The Merckx-Maertens antagonism took its predictable course when, Maertens says, Merckx offered 100,000 francs to him and to anyone who'd help him win the championship. Maertens refused and told reporters: "I will simply not ride for Merckx." That upset Merckx's fans so much that, according to Maertens, they threw cold water over his legs six times as the race went on.

Nevertheless he got into the front group with Merckx (on Campagnolo), Luis Ocaña (on a Spanish Campagnolo look-alike brand called Zeus) and Felice Gimondi (also on Campagnolo). Merckx was the favorite, but Gimondi was no slouch, and Ocaña had won that year's Tour de France. Unlike many other World Championships, the title was to be decided by the big stars of the day. Of the four, Maertens was the least prestigious, but by far the best sprinter.

His version is that, though his legs had been cramping from the cold-water torture and his morale damaged by taunting and jeering from the crowd, he was enough of a danger to Merckx to be worth a decent offer. In one version he is said to have remembered: "He said that if I led him out in the sprint, there had be a pile of gold waiting for me." Certainly in his biography, *Niet van horen zeggen* (literally, *"Not Just Hearsay,"* translated under the title *Fall from Grace*), he accepts that he had agreed to let Merckx win and to lead him out in the sprint.

Maertens continued: "I started the sprint from a long way out. Just like he'd asked me to. Why from a long way out? It's obvious now: I was supposed to blow up. Merckx got on my wheel. I was looking out, waiting, wondering where he'd got to, still waiting, but he didn't come. Only then did I realize that I had been knifed in the back by Merckx and that because his own chance had gone, he would have rather see the Italian win on a Campagnolo-equipped bike than me.

"Once over the finish line and seething with anger, I shouted 'Coward!' at Merckx. Like an innocent choirboy he began to cry."

Needless to say, Merckx refutes the story and says the finish was just what it was seen to be, a good win for Gimondi and a disappointing day for him. But even allowing for Maertens' talent for seeing cloaked figures in every dark corner, the fact that such a story could gain currency shows the discredit in which World Championships and national teams can be held.

It probably explains the World Cup. Nobody in high places is likely to abandon the romance of a one-off World Championship or to run it for trade rather than national teams, which would reduce it to another race. But judging the world's best rider over a season of races as different as Paris–Roubaix and Milan–San Remo produces a more convincing result. And it's on that, rather than a rainbow jersey, that riders now negotiate their contract.

# Further Reading and Chapter Notes[*]

Readers who wish to further deepen their knowledge of the issues of stimulants and doping in cycling, and in sport in general, will find it to be a rich and complex subject to explore. Those who can read French will find an entire shelf of confessional and analytical books on the Festina affair and its implications available from French publishers via the Internet. The Festina affair and the disruptions in the 1998 Tour de France have certainly been the global stimulus for other sports to take a harder look at matters of health, legality, and fairness in the use of stimulants and doping products. And yet the question remains, how exactly should "doping" be defined? Which products and substances are allowable, when, and under what conditions? What is fair, and what exactly should be defined as "cheating"?

Recently, to answer the above questions, the World Anti-Doping Agency was formed, and has hammered out "The World Anti-Doping Code" [for the full text of that 52-page document, see http://www.wada.org], with which the Union Cycliste Internationale — with some reservations — is now in agreement. A World Anti Doping Conference was held in March 2003 in Copenhagen, and the WADA Code is intended to supercede the existing Olympic Movement Anti-Doping Code prior to the 2004 Athens Olympic Games, including strong sanctions against athletes who test positive in doping tests.

Readers who wish to further explore doping issues and general cycling history in the 19th century will have a more difficult search. Certainly, John Hoberman, *Mortal Engines: The Science of Performance and the Dehumanization of Sport* (New York: The Free Press, 1992) is essential reading — see particularly Chapter 4, "Faster, Higher, Stronger – A History of Doping in Sport," and his 50 pages of Bibliographic Notes. Since stimulants were more or less openly used and advocated in cycling in the 1890s (although the details were not necessarily known, as in the case of Choppy Warburton, see Chapter 1), there was little controversy surrounding them, and there were no arrests or doping trials which would have revealed the practices. Therefore, other than advertisements for cocaine-based proprietary products, the researcher will not find much discussion of doping issues in the cycling press in the 1890s.

Those tempted to explore general cycling history in the 1880s and 1890s, and who have access to a good library in a major city in Britain or the United States, will find a substantial number of English-language periodicals which covered the sport and the industry (for example, *The Cyclist, Bicycling News, Wheeling*, and *Cycling* in England, and *Bearings, The Referee*, and *Bicycling World* in the USA), and the same is true for French-language sources in France (where in the 1890s there were at least a dozen periodicals more or less entirely devoted to cycling matters). The daily newspapers of larger American cities were very interested in cycling in the 1890s, and many fascinating accounts of racing and the impact of cycling on urban social history can be uncovered by a patient researcher prepared to weather the frustrations of poorly maintained microfilm and microfiche machines.

---

[*]    Prepared by Andrew Ritchie and Rob van der Plas

## Chapter 1

For Choppy Warburton, Jimmy Michael, and the Linton brothers, information is scattered and sketchy in period literature (see remarks on page 181).

For the emerging relationship between professional racers and professional managers,and general background material on racing in the 1890s see:
Ritchie, Andrew: *Major Taylor: The Extraordinary Career of a Champion Bicycle Racer.* San Francisco, Bicycle Books, 1988 (original hardcover edition) and Baltimore: Johns Hopkins University Press, 1996. (paperback edition).

A French-language source for this period is:
Durry, Jean: *La véridique histoire des géants de la route.* Freiburg (Switzerland): Denoël, 1973.

## Chapter 2

The most comprehensive source on Terront, in French, is:
Baudry de Saunier, Louis: *Les mémoires de Terront.* Paris: 1893 [this work was distributed at that year's 1,000 km race in Paris, where all 1,000 copies of the first printing were sold]. Reprint edition available from Paris: Prosport, 1980.

An English-language source on Terront is:
Ritchie, Andrew: "The Cycling World of Paris in 1893." *The Boneshaker* 143 (Spring 1997), pp. 12–23.

A source for Paris–Brest–Paris is:
Ritchie, Andrew: Charles Terront and Paris–Brest–Paris in 1891, *The Boneshaker* 150 (Summer 1999), pp 9–20.

## Chapter 3

A good general source for the beginnings of six-day racing in the US is:
Meinert, Charles: Single Sixes in Madison Square Garden," *Proceedings of the 7th International Cycling History Conference, pp. 57–64.* San Francisco: Van der Plas Publications, 1997.

A source for this period, and the source of some of the quotes in this chapter is:
McGurn, James: *On Your Bicycle: An Illustrated History of Cycling.* New York, Oxford: Facts on File Publications, 1987 and London: John Murray, 1987.

For the information regarding Major Taylor, see:
Ritchie, Andrew: *Major Taylor: The Extraordinary Career of a Champion Bicycle Racer.* San Francisco, Bicycle Books, 1988 and Baltimore: Johns Hopkins University Press, 1996 (paperback edition).

Concerning six-day races being "de facto experiments," see:
Hobermann, John: *Mortal Engines: The Science of Performance and the Dehumanization of Sport,* New York: The Free Press, 1992, p. 13.

For the US tour of Cann and Terront, see:
Ritchie, Andrew: "The Beginnings of Trans-Atlantic Racing." *Proceedings of the 8th International Cycling History Conference,* pp. 131–142. San Francisco: Van der Plas Publications, 1998.

For Berretrot account, available only in French, see:
  Berretrot, George: *Minuit, l'heure des primes*. Paris: Fournier-Valdes, 1950.

For more recent 6-day racing, see:
  Harper, Ted: *Six Days of Madness*. Stroud, Canada: Pacesetter Press, 1993.

For some of the comments on early 6-day racing, see also:
  McGurn (see Chapter 2 notes for details) and Ritchie, 1988 (see Chapter 1 notes for details)

For more on Hassenforder (in French), see:
  Ollivier, Jean-Paul: *La véridique histoire de Roger Hassenforder*. Paris: Glénat, 1999.

## Chapter 4

The first official International Cyclists' Association World Championships were held in Chicago in 1893.

For the formation of the ICA, see:
  "Formation of the International Cyclists' Association." *The Scottish Cyclist*, 13 Nov. 1892.

For Paris–Roubaix reference, see:
  Sergeant, Pascal: *A Century of Paris–Roubaix*, London: Bromley Books, 1997.

## Chapters 5 and 6

Regarding Simpson quotes, see:
  Simpson, Tom: *Cycling is My Life. London: Stanley Paul*, 1966.

French-language sources for the other subject matter covered in these chapters include:
  Chany, Pierre: *La fabuleuse histoire du cyclisme*. Paris: ODIL, 1975

  Chany, Pierre: *La fabuleuse histoire des grandes classiques et des championnats du monde*. Paris: ODIL, 1979.

For the Pellisier brothers, see:

  Bastide, Roger: *La legende des Pellisier*. Paris: Presses de la Cité, 1981.

Two autobiographical accounts for Anquetil are:
  Anquetil, Jacques: *Je suis comme ça*. Paris: Union Générale d'editions, 1964.

  Anquetil, Jacques: *En brulant des étapes*. Paris: Calman-Levy, 1966.

Two additional Anquetil biographies are:
  Chany, Pierre, and Anquetil, Janine: *Anquetil*. Paris: Hatier, 1971.

  Ollivier, Jean-Paul: *La véridique histoire de Jacques Anquetil*. Paris: Glénat, 1994.

For Lapébie, see:
  Ollivier, Jean-Paul: *La véridique histoire de Roger et Guy Lapébie*. Paris: Glénat, 2000. (By the same author, published in the same series, are biographies of many of the men mentioned here and elsewhere in this book.)

## Chapter 7

For Simpson anecdotes and other recollections, see Simpson (1966), previously referenced.

For the Wagtmans v. Walkowiak account, a French-language source is:
  Ollivier, Jean-Paul: *Le Maillot Jaune assassiné – Roger Walkowiak*. Paris: Glénat.

## Chapter 8

For French- (and Dutch-) language information on Trousellier and Garrigou, see:
  Nelissen, Jean: *La bible du Tour de France/ De Bijbel van de Tour de France*. Maastricht (NL): WIN Publications, 1995 (This is also a source for "potted biographies" of all other Tour de France winners until 1994).

For Berretrot account, in French, see: Berretrot (1950), previously referenced.

Bernard Sainz, or "Dr. Mabuse" has written his own account, in which he defends his actions in the following French-language work:
  Sainz, Bernard: *Les stupéfiantes révélations du Dr. Mabuse*. Paris: J.C. Lattès, 2000.

Monthéour's account can be found in the following French-language source:
  Monthéour, Erwann: *Secret défonce – ma vérité sur le dopage*. Paris: J.C. Lattès, 1999.

For Willy Voet's account in English see:
  Voet, Willy: *Breaking the Chain: Drugs and Cycling – The True Story*. London: Yellow Jersey, 2001. (original French edition published by Calmann-Lévi, 1999)

## Chapter 9

For Menthéour reference, see:
  Menthéour (1999), previously referenced.

For Olympics reference, see:
  Killanin, Lord, and John Redda: *Olympic Games – 80 Years of People, Events and Records*. London: Barre & Jenkins, 1971, 1976.

The Simpson episode has become a much-publicized event in light of the 1998 Festina affair. For more information on this subject, see:
  Fotheringham, William: *Put Me Back on My Bike – In Search of Tom Simpson*. London: Yellow Jersey Press, 2002. (At the time of this writing, this is the most thorough and unbiased book on the subject available in English)

  Sidwells: *Mr. Tom – the True Story of Tom Simpson*. Norwich: Mousehold Press, 2000.

  Simpson (1966), previously referenced.

  Ollivier, Jean-Paul: *Simpson, un champion dans la tourmente*. Paris: Glénat, 2002.

For information about Roger Rivière (in French), see:
  Ollivier, Jean-Paul: *La tragedie du Parjoure: Roger Riviére*. Paris: Glénat, 1992.

For the writings of Blondin, see:
  Blondin, Antoine: *Sur le Tour de France*. Paris: Hachette, 1977.

For Poulidor (in French), see:
> Laborde, Christian: *Duel sur le volcane*. Paris: Michel Albin: 1998.

> Ollivier, Jean-Paul: *La véridique histoire de Raymond Poulidor*. Paris: Glénat, 1994.

## Chapter 10

For a general overview of the history of doping in bicycle racing, see:
> Rabenstein, Ruediger: "Some Facts About the History of Doping in Cycling Competition. *Proceedings of the 8th International Cycling History Conference*, Glasgow. San Francisco: Van der Plas Publications, 1998.

For more information on the Belgian drug tests, refer to the following Dutch-language source:
> Clarijs, J.P. and R.G.J. van Ingen Schenau (Eds.): *Wielrennen – Een confrontatie tussen de wetenschap en de praktijk van het wielrennen*. Lochem (NL), Gent (B): De Tijdstroom, 1985.

For the David Saunders quotes, see:
> Saunders, David: *Cycling in the Sixties*. London: Pelham Books, 1971.

For more on the Maertens account, see:
> Maertens, Freddy and Manu Adriaens: *Fall from Grace*. Hull: Ronde Publications, 1993. (Original Dutch-language edition: Antwerpen: Standaard Uitgeverij, 1988.

For Anquetil, see:
> Yates, Richard: *Master Jacques – the Enigma of Jacques Anquetil*. Norwich: Mousehold Press, 2001, and the following previously referenced works:

> Ollivier, Jean-Paul (1994).

> Anquetil, Jecques (1964).

> Anquetil, Jacques (1966).

> Channy, Pierre, and Anquetil, Janine (1971).

For Simpson, see Simpson references previously referenced for Chapter 9.

## Chapter 11

For Goddet, in French, see:
> Marchand, Jacques: Jacques Goddet. Paris: Atlantica, 2002.

For Pollentier references, see:
> Maertens (1993), previously referenced.

## Chapter 12

For Voet account, see:
> Voet (2001), previously referenced.

For Monthéour account, see also:
> Monthéour (1999), previously referenced.

## Chapter 13

For Monthéour, see also:
Monthéour (1999), previously referenced.

For Patrick Laure, an important writer on doping issues in French, see among other titles:
Laure, Patrick: *Le dosier de dopage*. Paris: Excelsior, 1999.

For Virenque, in French, see:
Virenque, Richard: *Ma vérité*. Paris: Editions du Rocher, 1999.

Versini, Jean-Paul: *Richard Virenque plus fort qu'avant*. Paris: Robert-Lafont, 2002.

## Chapter 14

For van Steenbergen, in French, see:
Ollivier, Jean-Paul: *La véridique histoire de Rik van Steenbergen*. Paris: Glénat, 2000.

For general background on the Festina affair and doping use in general see:
Voet (2001), previously referenced.

Voet, Willy: *Cinquante ans de Tours pendable*. Paris: Flammarion, 2002.

Guillon, Nicholas, and J.f. Quénet: *Un cyclone nommé dopage – les secrets du dossier Festina*. Paris: Editions Solar, 1999.

Roussel, Bruno: *Tour de vices*. Paris: Hachette, 2001.

For Virenque's account, see:
Virenque (1999), previously referenced.

## Chapter 15

For some of the anecdotal references in this chapter, see:
Simpson (1966).

For the LeMond v. Boyer incident, see:
Abt, Samuel: *In High Gear – The World of Professional Bicycle Racing*. San Francisco: Bicycle Books, 1989, 1990.

Abt, Samuel: *LeMond – The Incredible Comeback of an American Hero*. New York: Random House, 1990.

For van Steenbergen, see:
Ollivier (2000), previously referenced

In this context also see:
Maertens & Adriaens (1993), previously referenced.

# Index

criterium racing, 99–100, 118
and doping, 100, 118
Crowe, Kevin, 126
Crystal Palace track, 20
*Cyclers' News*, 14, 19
"Cycling Doctor," 20, 21 (*see also*
Turner, Dr. E. B.)
*Cycling Gazette*, 11
Cyclist versus horse race, in
Agricultural Hall, 24
cyclists as guinea pigs, 150

**D**

Dauphiné Libéré, 87
de Gaulle, Charles, and "les
évenements de '68," 130
de Merode, Prince Alexandre,109,
145
on doping controls, 109
on medical profession as
source of drugs, 145
de Montbrial, Thibault, 155
de Pauw, Noel, 127
Da Pra, Tommaso, 112
de Schaepdryver, Prof., 116
de Vleeschouwer, Prof., 116
De Wilde, Roger, and drug use,
127
Defillipis, Nino, 173
Delblat, Louis, 47, 81
Deloor, Gustave, 66
Demuysere, Jef, 71
Denmark, and 1931 World
Championship, 56
Denson, Vin, 87, 90–91, 171
and urinating, 90
"*départ réel*," 83
Derny, and pacing, 86–90
Derny, Roger, 89
descending, v. climbing, 82
Desgrange, Henri, 31–32, 61–65,
67, 71–72, 93
Desmet, Gilbert, 73
Dhaenens, Pierre, judge at doping
trial, 127
Dirix, Dr. André, 109, 113,
117–118, 120, 126
on doping controls., 109
and drug use at 1967 World
Championships, 126
Dolman, Eef, 123, 132
and cheating at drug tests, 123

doping, 15, 18–20, 103–114,
115–127, 129–134, 136–139,
141–147, 149–163
estimated deaths, 113
introduction of new drugs, 117
and social attitude to, 116
used to slow down a rider, 18
in cycling v. other sports,
103–104
doping controls, 115, 121–124
cheating at, 121–123
cost of, 115
introduction of, 115
selection of riders to test, 132
doping experiment, 39
Dortignacq, Jean-Baptiste, 62
Dousset, Daniel, 98–99, 113
"Dr. Punto," (*see* Rijckaert, Erik)
drug raids, 110–111, 116
drugs (*see also* doping, drug
raids), 11--117, 130–138, 150
secondary effects of, 150
social use of, 130–138
Duboc, Paul, 62
Duffield, David, 119

Dumas, Dr. Pierre, 76, 108–117,
130–131, 145
and doping controls, 108
Dunlop, 17, 31–32
Durand, Jacky, 66
Duvallet, Dr. Alain, and drug
availability, 143

**E**

"Eagle of Hoogerheide," (*see*
Ottenbros, Harm)
earnings, of professional cyclists,
95
Eastern Europe, as source of
drugs, 143
*Economic History Services*, 39, 73
Egli, Paul, 172
Elliott, Shay, 169, 175
and World Championship, 169
England, as opposed to Britain, 50
(*see also* Great Britain)
Ephedrine, 118
EPO, 142–147, 152, 163
availability of, 144
detection of, 146
function explained, 142
in Voet's possession, 152
quality of, 144

sources of, 143
use in Italy v. France, 142
Epogen, (*see* EPO)
erythropoietin, (*see* EPO)
"Eternal Second," (*see* Poulidor,
Raymond)
Etherington, Barry, 40
*extra-sportif*, sponsor, 168

**F**

Faber, François, 64
Faema team, 178
Faggin, Leandro, 126
Falk Hansen, Willie, 53–54
Festina Affair, 104, 149–163
Filmer, Martin, 126
fish poisoning v. drugs, 76
fixing, of race results, 45
Flandria team, 172
*flechette*, explained, 101
France, government of, and
Festina affair, 156
Franco- Prussian war, 29
Franco–Belgian rivalry, 67
Franco-Italian rivalry, 70
"free drink trick," 95
"free meal trick," 94–95
Frigo, Dario, and Giro drug raid,
162

**G**

Galérie des Machines, 28
Garin, César, 31
Garin, Rudolphe, 31
Garin. Maurice, 62
Garrigou, Gustave, 62–64
*Gazzetta dello Sport*, 71
Géminiani, Raphaël, 88, 106, 168
on Nencini, 106
Georget, Léon, 31
Ghent– Wevelgem, 171
Giffard, Pierre, 29, 31 (*see also*
Paris–Brest–Paris)
Gimondi, Félice, 178–179
Giro d'Italia, drug raid, 162–163
Gladiator, 16
Goddet, Jacques, 83, 111, 131
on doping controls, 131–133
on rider protest strike, 111
Golebiewski, Wlodzimierz, 69, 108
on Enemark's death, 108
Goullet. Alf, 41
Gowland, Tony, 47, 139

## Our books…
are available in book shops and Internet stores via our trade distributors in the US, Canada, the UK, and Australia, as well as in selected bike shops. If you should encounter problems locating any of our books, or want to request a catalogue, please visit our web site or contact us by telephone or in writing:

### Cycle Publishing
1282 7th Avenue
San Francisco, CA 94122, USA
Tel: (415) 665-8214; toll-free: 1-877-353-1207; Fax: (415) 753-8572
E-mail: pubrel@cyclepublishing.com
Web site: http://www.cyclepublishing.com